Essays on Uzbek History, Culture, and Language

Indiana University Uralic and Altaic Series
Denis Sinor, Editor
Volume 156

Essays on
Uzbek History, Culture, and Language

EDITED BY

Bakhtiyar A. Nazarov
and
Denis Sinor

WITH

Devin DeWeese, technical editor

Indiana University
Research Institute for Inner Asian Studies
Bloomington, Indiana
1993

Library of Congress Catalog Card Number: 92-063232
ISBN: 0933070-29-2

Printed in the United States of America

CONTENTS

INTRODUCTION

The idea of a joint Uzbek-American volume of essays focusing on Uzbek history, literature and language arose in a conversation between Bakhtiyar A. Nazarov and Denis Sinor at the 30th annual meeting of the Permanent International Altaistic Conference (PIAC), held in Bloomington, Indiana in the summer of 1987. Beyond its scholarly aims it was meant to bear witness to the desirability and possibility of direct cooperation between scholars of the Soviet Socialist Republic of Uzbekistan and the United States.

Familiar with the often slow advance of cooperative projects with the Soviets - always hampered by inadequate communications - I was pleasantly surprised when one year later, in Weimar, on the last day of the 31st PIAC meeting, Professor Nazarov handed me the manuscripts of the Uzbek contributions to this volume. Elated, I did not realize at once that - because of their unidiomatic English - these articles were unpublishable in the form I received them. I turned for help to my younger colleague Professor Devin DeWeese and we reached the conclusion that without seeing the original Russian or Uzbek versions, there was no way to render into proper English the Uzbek contributions. It took some considerable time to obtain the originals, which were then translated into English by Devin DeWeese. It was a difficult and wearisome task which had to be accomplished simultaneously with other, more urgent activities, such as teaching. The two other editors are greatly indebted to Professor DeWeese for his most generous and selfless help, which extended also to the technical production of this volume.

Throughout, communications between Tashkent and Bloomington have remained slow and cumbersome. There were also a number of misunderstandings, and so it happened that what would have been Professor Nazarov's own contribution to this volume appeared in *Aspects of Altaic Civilization III* (ed. Denis Sinor, Indiana University Uralic and Altaic Series, vol. 145, 1990).

There are more than four American scholars interested in matters Uzbek. I approached most, perhaps even all of them. Some have never replied to the invitation, some declined it, others have never delivered the promised contributions. We had to go ahead without them.

The tremendous political changes which have taken place between the inception of the idea of producing this volume and its realization have not invalidated its original aim. It is a testimony of cordial relationships and effective cooperation between Uzbek and American scholars, each of whom, in his own way, attempts to shed some light on questions of past or present Uzbek history, culture, or language.

January 1993 Denis Sinor

THE ETHNOGENESIS OF THE UZBEK PEOPLE AND THE FORMATION OF THE UZBEK LANGUAGE

G. A. Abdurakhmanov

The formation of the language of any people is directly connected with the history of the origin and formation of that people. For this reason the study of the Uzbek people's ethnogenesis, is impossible without the joint effort of historians, ethnographers, linguists, archaeologists and the representatives of other adjunct disciplines. The question of the ethnogenesis of the Uzbek people requires the investigation of the history of ancient tribes which inhabited Central Asia (from the first millennium B.C.), such as the Saka or Shaka, the Massagetae, the Sogdians, peoples referred to according to their dwelling places (such as the Bactrians, Khorezmians, and natives of Chach and Parkent), and peoples of Turkic and non-Turkic origin inhabiting the regions neighboring Central Asia.[1]

The ethnogenesis of every people is determined by many factors, including the social structure within which a particular ethnic collectivity lives, its biological, psychological, cultural, and linguistic characteristics, etc.; the influence of related and unrelated peoples must also be considered, and the development and formation of a given people must be traced and determined in stages.

One of the most complex questions in determining the origin of the Uzbek people and the formation of the Uzbek language is the study of the earliest history of Central Asia and the identification of the most ancient ethnic groups inhabiting this region.[2] As historical material for studying this question may be mentioned Iranian, Greek, Latin, Chinese, Turkic, Arabic, and Persian written sources (e.g. the *Avesta* of the first millennium B.C., Achaemenid inscriptions on

[1] Such tribes are mentioned in Greek, Persian, Indian, Chinese, and Arabic sources.

[2] The question of the linguistic affiliation of the ethnic groups inhabiting ancient Central Asia remains controversial. Maḥmūd Kāshgharī in the second half of the 11th century affirmed that in his time no one speaking Sogdian alone remained in this area, that the majority of people spoke Turkic, and that many spoke both Turkic and Sogdian. However, he did not discuss the Sogdian language's relation to either Persian or Turkic.

stone, brick, leather, and papyrus, the works of Herodotus, Ktesias, Xenophon, and Ptolemy), as well as certain archeological excavations, dialectological materials, and the analysis of personal, geographic, and ethnic names. The oldest written sources date back only to the beginning of the 5th century B.C.

It is known that the most ancient people (8th-2nd centuries B.C.) of Central Asia consisted of the Scythians (according to Greek sources) or Saka (in Persian sources), the Massagetes, the Sogdians, Khorezmians, and other ethnic groups. For example, the Massagetes inhabited the lower courses of the Amu Darya and Syr Darya, while the Saka dwelled in the territory of Kazakhstan in the southern and eastern parts of Central Asia as far as the Altay; in the oases of Tashkent and Khorezm, as well as in the Farghana valley and in most of the territory of Sogdiana lived Turkic ethnic groups (the Kangüy or Qangli), some of whom formed the state of Kangha or Kangüy (2nd century B.C to 1st century A.D.).

The conquest of Central Asia by Alexander the Great in 329-327 B.C., and the 150 years of Greco-Macedonian rule which followed, had no influence upon the ethnic composition or language of the local population.

The second stage of formation of the Uzbek people is connected with the penetration of Turkic ethnic groups from East - the Yüeh-chih (or Kushans, or Tokharians, 3rd-2nd centuries B.C.), the Huns (2nd-4th centuries A.D.), and the Hephthalite tribes (5th-6th centuries A.D.) As a result of this, as is well known, the Kushans formed their own state, as did the Hephthalites after them. At the head of the Kushan state stood one of the five Yüeh-chih clans, the "Guishuan" (Kushan); this state held Central Asia, Afghanistan, and part of India. It is unclear whether Khorezm, Sogdiana, or Chach were included in the Kushan state.

In written sources it is noted that the aforementioned tribes or confederations were Turkic-speaking; the ethnic composition of the Hephthalites is not indicated, but their close relation to the Huns is mentioned. "O. I. Smirnova's research on the Sogdian coins from Panjikent convincingly demonstrates that many of the representatives of the ruling dynasties of Sogdiana came from Turkic tribes."[3]

[3] Cf. *Istoriia Uzbekskoi SSR* (Tashkent, 1967), p. 200.

During the 6th-8th centuries A.D. various Turkic tribes from Kazakhstan, Kirghizstan, Semirechye, and other neighboring regions penetrated into present-day Uzbekistan and assimilated with the native population. This period may be termed the period of the Turkic qaghanate, with Central and Inner Asia included in its territory. As is known, in 588 the Turkic qaghanate was divided into eastern and western qaghanates, with centers in Mongolia and Semirechye, respectively. In the western qaghanate lived the tribal and nominal confederation of the Qarluqs, Khalaj, Qangli, Türgesh, Chigil, and Oghuz; eventually the Oghuz split with this union and formed their own state. In the eastern *qaghanate* the Uyghurs ruled at that time.

In 745 the Turkic qaghanate was overthrown by the Uyghurs, who then formed the Uyghur state which survived down to 840; then it was destroyed by the Khakas (Qirghiz). As a result, part of the Uyghurs joined the Qarluqs, part migrated to Tibet, while the rest remained in the Altay and mixed with other Turkic groups.

In the 8th century Central Asia was conquered by the Arabs. Under Arab rule Bukhara, Samarqand, Qarshi, and Shahrisabz were inhabited by Sogdians, while Qarluqs dwelled in the Farghana valley and other Turkic tribes (including the Türgesh) nomadized in the vast territory of Central Asia and present-day Kazakhstan. The noted historian aṭ-Ṭabarī noted that the chiefs of the Sogdians were Turks.

During the 9th-10th centuries Central Asia was ruled by the Samanids,[4] under whom Arabic remained the language of state administration and of learning; the ordinary, conversational language was the language of various Turkic tribes. In the 10th-11th centuries power shifted to the Qarakhanids, whose state split in the mid-11th century into eastern and western halves, with centers in Balasaghun (later Kashghar) and Uzgand (later Samarqand), respectively. The eastern half included East Turkestan, Semirechye, Shash, Farghana, and ancient Sogdiana, while the western half inlcuded Afghanistan and northern Iran. At the same time the Ghaznavid state, founded by

[4] Saman, ancestor of the Samanids, was a feudal lord from Balkhaw, which according to some sources was among the outlying areas of Samarqand; he was a governor under Ṭāhir b. Ḥusayn, who in 821 was appointed by the Caliph as governor of Khurāsān (which included Mawarannahr as well). In 888 the Samanid dynast Ismāʿīl became independent ruler of Mawarannahr and eastern Iran.

Maḥmūd Ghaznavī, formed in Khurāsān and lasted until 1040, when it was overthrown by the Turkmen tribes of the Seljüks. Ghaznavid territory stretched from northern India to the southern shore of the Caspian sea, including present-day Afghanistan and northern Iran. Khorezm, meanwhile, because of its geographical situation, was not originally part of either the Qarakhanid or the Ghaznavid state; nevertheless, it was conquered by the Ghaznavids in 1017.

The Qarakhanid state was formed by the tribal confederation of the Qarluq, Yaghma, and Chigil; when the state split into two parts the connections of Mawarannahr with East Turkestan and Semirechye weakened. However, historians have rightly noted that "it would be incorrect to contrast Mawarannahr as a sedentary, Sogdian world, with Semirechye as a nomadic, Turkic world."[5] To begin with, there is no substantial proof that the Sogdians spoke an Indo-European language, while on the other hand, as noted, Maḥmūd Kāshgharī does not connect the Sogdian language to any Turkic dialect known to him. The testimony of the historian Ṭabarī, and the results of O. I. Smirnov's studies on Sogdian coins, show that the Sogdian language was close to the Turkic and that Turkic tribes played a decisive role in the life of the Sogdian tribes. Be that as it may, as the sources attest, Turkic tribes were the primary and leading elements in Mawarannahr and Semirechye. The settlement of more and more Turkic tribes strengthened the position and language of the Turkic tribes inhabiting that territory, and they could not help but influence the language and ethnic composition of the Sogdian tribes.

From the 8th century, the chief tribes in Farghana were the Qarluqs, while in Shash the Oghuz predominated. The Sogdians, inhabiting the small territories between the Turkic tribes, "gradually lost their ethnic particularity, as they intermarried with the Turks; and the Sogdians likewise lost their own language, replacing it with Turkic."[6]

In the 10th and 11th centuries, the chief group of the Oghuz lived along the lower Syr Darya, later moving into the territory of present-

[5] *Istoriia Uzbekskoi SSR*, t. I, p. 346.

[6] Cf. *Istoriia Uzbekistana*, t. I, p. 348; "the same process occurred in Khorezm, where the settlement of nomadic Oghuz and Qipchaq tribes endid, according to V. V. Bartol'd, in the 13th century with the virtually complete disappearance of the former Khorezmian language" (*ibid.*, p. 498).

day Turkmenistan. In Semirechye the major tribe, the Qarluqs, from the Talas valley to East Turkestan, with the Chigil tribe inhabiting the region northeast of Issyk Kul, the Yaghma tribe (or tribal union) south of Issyk Kul and in East Turkestan, and the Türgesh (or the Tukhsi and Arghu) dwelling in southwestern Semirechye. Maḥmūd Kāshgharī considered the Türgesh (Tukhsi and Arghu) language to be mixed with Sogdian; evidently the mutual influences of these tribes were strong.

At the beginning of the 12th century, Central Asia was conquered by the Qarakhitay from the east. There are diverse opinions as to the ethnic composiiton of the Qarakhitay, some considering them to be of Tunguz origin, others of Mongol origin. They left no trace whatsoever either ethnically or linguistically in Central Asia; after their defeat of the Seljük Sanjar and the Qarakhanid Maḥmūd, they limited their role to the collection of tribute.

From the first half of the 13th century to the second half of the 14th (that is, from 1219 to 1370), the peoples of Central Asia were under the rule of the Mongols, followed by the period of Timurid rule down to the end of the 15th century. But it must be emphasized that the Arabs, Persians, and Mongols who ruled Central Asia in these historical periods were not able to exert any effect on the ethnic structure or language of the indigenous population, although the Arabic and Persian languages were adopted in those times as the languages of court and scholarship.

Following the dissolution of the Golden Horde beginning in the 14th century, and with the decay of the Timurid statte in the second half of the 15th century, the state of the nomadic Uzbeks formed in the 1420s as a result of the internecine wars in the eastern part of the Dasht-i Qipchaq, which encompassed the territory from the Volga eastwards as well as the regions north of the Syr Darya (including the territory of present-day Kazakhstan and southwestern Siberia). The founder of this state was Abū'l-Khayr Khan, whose grandson, Muḥammad Shaybānī Khan,[7] ended the power of the Timurids and

[7] The tribes of Shībān, grandson of Chingiz Khan, assimilated with the local Turkic tribes and adopted their language and customs, undergoing changes in their ethnic composition. The Uzbek tribes were likewise not unified ethnically, but formed in the steppe out of various ancient tribes such as the Saka, Massagetae, Huns, and other Turkic and Mongol tribes.

continued his conquests to become ruler of the territory from the Syr Darya to Afghanistan.

The decay of the Shaybanid state, or rather of its continuator the Ashtarkhanid state, began under the khan ʿUbaydullāh II (1702-1711); gradually Farghana, then Khorezm, and Balkh, were detached from it. After the brief rule of Nadir Shah (1740-1747) in Central Asia, three states were centralized: in Bukhara (the Manghït tribe), in Khiva (the Qungrats), and in Qoqand (the Mings). In this period the principal ordinary language was Uzbek, and literary and scholarly works were written in Uzbek, while Tajik was adopted as the language of state chanceries. In Samarqand and Bukhara both Tajik and Uzbek were spoken.

As a whole, the Turko-Mongol tribes which nomadized in the eastern part of the Dasht-i Qipchaq during the second half of the 14th century were called Uzbeks, and their territory was termed the land of the Uzbeks. After their conquest of Mawarannahr at the beginning of the 16th century, the local population there also began to be called Uzbeks; in other words, without exerting any substantial influence upon the ethnic composition of the local native population, these tribes contributed only their ethnonym, "Uzbek." It is possible that the great tribal confederations of the Uzbeks, as they intermingled with the local tribes, not only adopted the culture of the local population, but introduced their own customs and influenced their physical type.

As a personal anthroponym, the name "Uzbek" is encountered in the works of Nasavī, Juvaynī, and Rashīd ad-Dīn (13th century). Rashīd ad-Dīn mentions, for example, a prince Uzbek, son of Mingqudar and grandson of Bukal, the seventh son of Jöchi. It must be noted that Uzbek Khan was the khan of the Golden Horde, but that the nomadic Uzbeks were not subject to him. There were other figures named "Uzbek" before Uzbek Khan; in particular, this name was borne by one of the *atabeks* of the Ildegizid dynasty (1210-1225) and by one of the *amīrs* of the Khorezmshah Muḥammad (1200-1220).

Here we may note also that the ancient tribes of the Saka, Massagetae, Sogdians, Khorezmians, and Turks, as well as other ethnic groups who joined with them somewhat later, were the base of formation not only of the Uzbeks, Kazakhs, Kirghiz, Karakalpaks, Uyghurs, and other Turkic peoples, but participated as well in the formation of the neighboring Tajik people.

And it must be remembered also that one and the same tribe or clan might contribute in the formation of various Turkic peoples. For example, within both the Uzbek and Kazakh peoples are clans of Qipchaqs, Jalayirs, Naymans, and Kattaghans. Thus, the fact that common features exist in the Uzbek and Kazakh languages should not be considered the result of later linguistic contacts on the part of these peoples.

In summary, the rule of the ancient Turks in Central Asia comprises the period from the 5th-10th centuries, and the succeeding dynasties did not effect any changes in the ethnic composition of the Turkic population inhabiting the enormous territory (in Inner Asia, southern Siberia, Kazakhstan, Central Asia, East Turkestan, etc.); the language, customs, dress, culture, and other features of the Turkic ethnic groups continued to remain quite close and similar.

As a rule, each Turkic qaghanate formed out of a distinctive ethnic group, and each ethnic group was called by the name of one of the highly privileged clans or tribes, although in its composition were found a multitude of other clans and tribes. For example, within the Qarluq ethnic group existed, beyond the Qarluqs themselves, the Chigils (chiefly in Mawarannahr) and Yaghma (from the Ili valley to Kāshghar); and the Yaghma, prior to their amalgamation with the Qarluqs, were found within the ethnic structure of the Toquz Oghuz. A similar situation is observed in the case of the Uyghur ethnic group. For this reason, such an ethnic group might appear as the basis of formation for various Turkic-speaking peoples; for example, from the Uyghur ethnic group formed not only the contemporary Uyghurs, but the Uzbeks, Kazakhs, Kirghiz, etc. And the same may be noted concerning literary monuments: some of these, conditionally termed "Uyghur," relate to the history of formation not only of the Uyghur language, but of other contemporary Turkic languages as well, since their speakers' ancestors were included in the ancient Uyghur ethnic structure.

In the 11th century major Turkic unions formed in Central Asia, Kazakhstan, and western Siberia: the Oghuz in the south, the Qarluq and Uyghur in the east, and the Qipchaq in the west and northwest; this is of course conditional, inasmuch as each of these united within it tens of other smaller ethnic groups. The state language would be determined by which tribe occupied the dominant position in a given period.[8]

It is well known that the colloquial, conversational language precedes the literary language; as a rule, the language of the more privileged, ruling clan or tribe would begin to perform the function of a written and common language, while the languages of the remaining clans or tribes, amounting to dialects, would be preserved in colloquial speech.

The process of the unification of the various ethnic groups and the rapprochement of their languages occurred simultaneously with the rule of each of the states named above (i.e. the Kangu, Kushans, Hephthalites, Qarakhanids, etc.); this led to the formation and spread of a common language and to its adoption by diverse ethnic groups. And it must be noted also that the language of the literary monuments of the 6th-10th centuries is characterized by a relative uniformity, despite the frequent changes of ruling groups.

Maḥmūd Kāshgharī distinguished the Qipchaq, Oghuz, and Uyghur languages from one another; the Chigil group was at this time part of the Qarluq tribes, with which it had begun to assimilate. Kāshgharī considered the Oghuz dialect to be the most "elegant" language of that time, as well as the languages of the Yaghma and Tukhsi tribes; however, in his opinion the most "correct" (i.e. literary) language was the "Khāqānī" (which, according to Bartol'd, was the language of the Yaghma tribe).

During the period of Mongol rule in Central Asia the Mongol language and culture did not exert serious influences upon the local Turkic languages and cultures. On the contrary, several Mongol tribes (the Barlas, Jalayir, Qongrat, and others) were assimilated by Turkic tribes.

Thus one must not connect the contemporary Uzbek people only with the Uzbek tribes which in the 14th century became part of the tribal groups inhabiting Central Asia over the course of centuries. Numerous ancient ethnic groups noted above formed the basis of the Uzbek people; the process of their formation began in the 11th century, and was completed in the 14th century, from which time the

[8] According to Ibn Muhannā, a special linguistic treatise was composed in the Qanglï language.

ethnonym "Uzbek" solidified as their designation. But the small number of Uzbek tribes who came from the Dasht-i Qipchaq were only the last constituent element of the Uzbek people.[9]

The process of the separation of the Uzbek people from other Turkic peoples began in the 11th century and concluded in the 14th, and the formation of the Uzbek language belongs to the same period. The dialect structure of the contemporary Uzbek language also points to this complex historical process; the modern Uzbek language is formed on the basis of four groups of dialects - Samarkand-Bukhara, Tashkent, Fergana, and Khorezm - reflecting Qarluq-Uyghur, Oghuz, and Qipchaq linguistic features.

The primary sources for determining the periodization of the history of the Uzbek language are literary monuments written in the runic Turkic, Uyghur, and Sogdian alphabets; these are quite close to one another, although they have been discovered across an immense territory (in Mongolia, the Turfan oases, East Turkestan, eastern Siberia, Central Asia, Kazakhstan, the Altay, Khakasia, Tuva, Buryatia, and, even in the village of Nagyszentmiklós in Hungary, discovered in 1799). However, the languages of the literary sources written from the 12th to the 14th centuries show substantive differences: in some Qarluq-Uyghur features are found, in others Oghuz, and in yet others Qipchaq. Beginning from the end of the 14th century the linguistic features of literary monuments once again show common characteristics and differ only slightly from one another. This, of course, reflects the role of the socio-political factors of the age: the formation of a centralized state, as a rule, led to the unification of peoples and the convergence or integration of their languages, while the breakup of the state led to the fragmentation of peoples and the strengthening of the role of local dialects among them.

The classification and periodization proposed by various researchers in the history of the Turkic languages (and of Uzbek), such as S. E. Malov, A. N. Samoilovich, A. N. Kononov, A. M. Shcherbak, N. A. Baskakov, A. K. Borovkov, A. von Gabain, and others, have highlighted particular aspects of the issue and thereby complemented one another. On the basis of investigating the history of the forma-

[9] Cf. *Istoriia Uzbekskoi SSR*, t. I, pp. 501-507.

tion of the Uzbek people, and of analyzing the language of those who possess written monuments, it is possible to distinguish the following five periods in the process of the formation of the Uzbek language, each characterized by its own phonetic, lexical, and grammatical features:

I. THE MOST ANCIENT TURKIC LANGUAGE: the language formed in the period from most ancient times down to the formation of the Türk qaghanate (that is, down to the 6th century). Written records of the language of this period have not yet been discovered, rendering the determination of this period's chronological "borders" conditional. The languages of the ancient Saka, Massagetae, Sogdians, Kangüy, and other ethnic groups of this period are the original foundation for the formation of the contemporary Turkic languages of Central Asia and Kazakhstan, including Uzbek.

2. THE ANCIENT TURKIC LANGUAGE (6th-10th centuries): Literary monuments of this period were written in Runic, Uyghur, Sogdian, Manichaean, and Brahmi scripts, on stone (e.g. the Orkhon and Yenisei inscriptions) and on leather and special paper (found in Turfan). All these were produced in the period of the Turkic and Uyghur qaghanates and of Qirghiz rule.

The language of the Orkhon and Yenisei inscriptions (6th-10th centuries) represents a fully developed literary language with its own specific phonetic and grammatical characteristics and grammatical and stylistic norms. Therefore it is reasonable to suppose that this language and its written form underwent an extended period of development over several centuries, and this in turn leads to the idea that the process of the formation of the Old Turkic language was begun not in the period in which the above-named monuments were written, but much earlier. Consequently the formation of the old Turkic peoples was also underway many centuries before this period.

The linguistic tradition in question, with its grammatical and stylistic norms, is continued in the Uyghur written monuments of Turfan and elsewhere dating from the 8th to 13th centuries, in the monuments of the Qarakhanid period (10th-11th centuries), and so forth. The language of the Orkhon and Yenisei inscriptions and the Turfan texts was thus evidently the common language of all Turkic ethnic groups.

3. THE OLD TURKIC LANGUAGE (11th-14th centuries): This period is the most complex in the history of the formation of

Turkic languages; it was precisely in this period that the Uzbek, Kazakh, Kirgiz, Turkmen, Karakalpak, and other Turkic languages were formed. Professor A. M. Shcherbak calls the Turkic literary language of this period, in distinction from the Oghuz and Qipchaq languages, the language of East Turkistan.

Well-known works such as the *Qutadghu Bilig*, the *Dīwān lughāt at-turk*, *Hibat al-ḥaqā'iq*, the Quranic *tafsīr*, the *Oghuz-nāmah*, the *Qiṣaṣ al-anbiyā*, and others, were written in the Old Turkic language; nonetheless they bear linguistic features of diverse ethnic groups. Qarluq features are found in the *Qutadghu Bilig*, and Qipchaq (and less often Qangli and Qarluq) features in the *Oghuz-nāmah*, while the *Hibat al-ḥaqā'iq* represents somewhat of a transition between the Old Turkic and Old Uzbek languages.

4. THE OLD UZBEK LANGUAGE (14th-first half of the 19th centuries): At the beginning of the 14th century the Uzbek language diverged from other languages and began to function independently. Thus, for example, while characteristics of various Turkic languages in Central Asia may be traced in such works as the *Qutadghu Bilig*, the *Dīwān lughāt at-turk*, the *Oghuz-nāmah*, etc., in the works of the poets Sakkākī, Luṭfī, Durbek, and others written in the 14th century, together with the tradition of the Old Turkic language, one finds as the fundamental basis the linguistic features of the Qarluq-Uyghur ethnic groups, which participated in the formation of the Uzbek people. Similarly, in the language of the *Muḥabbat-nāmah* and the *Ta'ashshuq-nāmah* we find certain Oghuz features, while there are elements of the Qipchaq languages in *Khusraw va Shīrīn*; but in the language of the works of Navā'ī and Bābur, such dialectal elements are almost wholly lacking.

It is interesting to note that the works of Luṭfī, Sakkākī, Durbek, and others, written in the early period of the Old Uzbek language's [independent] functioning, display quite clearly the features of the living colloquial language of the Uzbeks; this language is well-understood by our contemporaries. 'Alī-shīr Navā'ī perfected this literary language in his works, enriching it with Arabic and Perso-Tajik linguistic media.[10] As a result, an original literary language

[10] Nevertheless, Bābur, in speaking about the language of Navā'ī's works, notes its closeness to the Andijan dialect; cf. *Babur-name*, ch. 1 (Tashkent), p. 18 (in Uzbek).

was formed, which over the course of several centuries served as an example and standard for other writers and poets. Only in the 17th and 18th centuries, in the works of Turdī, Abū'l-Ghāzī, and Gulkhānī, was this literary language somewhat simplified and brought closer to the living colloquial language.

5. THE NEW UZBEK LANGUAGE (from the second half of the 19th century): With the second half of the 19th century a literary language began to take shape which displayed all the characteristics of the living colloquial Uzbek language. This process was manifested in a departure from the tradition of the Old Uzbek literary language, in the rejection of archaic forms and elements, and in a closer reflection of the living language of the people; the process was especially activated during the 1920s. The phonetic structure of the contemporary Uzbek language is based on the Tashkent dialect, and its morphology on the Ferghana dialect.

A NEW ETHNIC TONE

IN WRITINGS FOR THE 21st CENTURY

Edward Allworth

Central political forces continue to push for reducing significant culture, artistic and social variation throughout the ethnic group spectrum in Central Asia.[1] The politicians work openly for full integration and homogeneity of the population while they strive steadily to eradicate many expressions of individual and ethnic group identity. That sense of specific nationality combines spoken or unspoken thoughts and feelings of a certain aggregate of people. In literature, that awareness includes communication both explicit and by implication. Ingrained ethnicity is so powerful that it can scarcely be neutralized in even the most eclectic, cosmopolitan writings, though it may not flaunt itself there.

Overt ethnic signals in imaginative writings - allusions to topography and onomasiology of a region or reference to sayings, traditional food or costume - appear still in some contemporary Soviet literature. But these days, the more potent manifestations of profound group identity must ordinarily be sought below the surface of an author's work. How may this singular ethnic voice be recognized in late twentieth-century literature? Perhaps best through apprehending the patterns of change emerging in subject matter, in quality of writing, in audience, in response to formal expectations (including extraliterary ones), and in the sustained sound of the writing. Rather than searching for origins of ethnic group consciousness, this study aims to detect the ongoing expression of national identity in current creative writing among Central Asian nationality authors' works (hereafter: Sovnatlit).

Central Asian literature in the USSR subsists in an environment quite different, in most respects, from the literary milieu beyond Soviet borders. Those surroundings probably affect new literature in a special way. It will be revealing and worthwhile not only to identify particulars of literary awareness but to compare some features

[1] "Nationality" designates only non-Russians, "ethnic" includes all such groups; "Central Asia" embraces the five union and one autonomous SSRs of the region.

of it among selected Central Asian nationalities and their writings. An abundance of publications in multiple copies is circulated annually for many of the USSR's ethnic groups. State publishing houses (private publishing is prohibited) regularly print books for more than 50 groups, and periodicals for more the 40 (eight of them Central Asian nationalities) in the indigenous languages. In 1979-82, they issued local-language materials for an average of 61 (books) and 45 (periodicals) groups, a small rise from the number served earlier. Central Asian literature came out with an annual average of at least 940 separate books and brochures in the various languages, including Russian, during 1979-82. Kazakhs and Uzbeks led the region with a yearly average of 315 and 212 such titles, respectively, in all languages. In the 1980s, the number of Central Asian literary titles is rising while the quantity of copies printed remains stable at about 26 million annually. This reflects growing activity among Central Asian writers. The record of publications in the same period for Azerbaijanian literature approximates that for the much more numerous Uzbeks.[2]

Such numbers dictate the method of selecting literature from representative groups. Five from among the largest Iranian and Turkic groups of the south have been chosen: Kazakh, Kirgiz, Tajik, Uzbek, and, for comparison, Azerbaijanian, each nationality with a population of around two million or more.[3] Original texts and translations, especially from anthologies and journals, all issued by Soviet publishing houses from the 1950s to the 1980s, provide all the specimens.

If literature from these five nationalities exhibits pervasive unity throughout, showing relatively little basic variety, this sampling may represent the entire Soviet category. If not, the problem of ethnic awareness may have to be solved for every single group separately,

[2] *Pechat' SSSR v 1979 godu. Statisticheskii sbornik* (Moscow: "Statistika," 1980), pp. 22-23, 63, 72-74; *Pechat' SSSR v 1980 godu. Stat. sb.* (Moscow: "Finansy i Statistika," 1981), pp. 24-25, 98, 106-108; *Pechat' SSSR v 1981 godu . . .* (1982), pp. 24-26, 98, 107-108; *Pechat' SSSR v 1982 godu . . .* (1983), pp. 24-25, 98, 107-109; Edward Allworth, "Mainstay or Mirror of Identity - the Printed Word in Central Asia and Other Soviet Regions Today," *Canadian Slavonic Papers*, 17/2-3 (1975), pp. 438, 454.

[3] *Naselenie SSSR. Po dannym Vsesoiuznoi perepisi naseleniia 1979 goda* (Moscow: Izdatel'stvo Politicheskoi Literatury, 1980), pp. 23-24.

or, for related clusters of nationalities. The rationale for selection thus becomes an integral part of the inquiry. And, the nature of significant differences, if any, between the nationalities in their transmission of group awareness through literature stands as a problem of real importance. To narrow the scope of the evidence and attain the objective of conceptualizing usefully about expression of nationality consciousness, the study examines one genre. All verse, as well as historical fiction, and such specialized genres as children's literature, science or space adventures, detective and spy stories will be excluded from consideration. Concentration upon stories and short novellas will give emphasis to current short prose writing about present or very recent subjects. Thus, the aim will be to ply the mainstream of forms, themes and styles of contemporary Sovnatlit taken largely from the Central Asian nationalities. The ultimate purpose of looking intently at this genre and the latest subjects is especially to discover some features of today's Sovnatlit that signal implicit nationality consciousness in the place and time selected. This will help to learn about the nature of the ethnic phenomenon in Sovnatlit generally. Finally, although the period chosen is relatively short - less than forty Christian years - the possibility must not be ignored that both the character and extent of enunciating awareness of nationality in literature may have altered since 1945. The Soviet literary system was noted until the mid-1950s, at least, for its tight state control of literature, and writing and criticism clearly reflected that situation. Now, there are indications that controls are applied somewhat differently, but the open intent of political authorities to harness literature to official policy purposes has not disappeared.

Amidst the many strong influences playing upon today's Sovnatlit, most noticeable must be the expectations of political and cultural ideologist. Expectations internalized by previous generations of Soviet authors have been passed on to posterity through the writings that survive them. This legacy also unquestionably affects the present writing in some way, though sponsored regulations and emphases have occasionally been revised. In Soviet literary life, "the demands" of the public, articulated through the statements of spokesmen for the sole political party, play a crucial role in guidance. One result of that procedure had been the creation of writings that may be regarded as strongly programmatic (advocating or following extraliterary guidelines or plans).

Official expectations, consequently, receive widespread attention in the press. They insure that the most striking trait of the many public literary discussions is the unwavering stress upon upbringing and edification rather than upon art and esthetics. In the sphere of nationality consciousness and how it is or is not to be treated, the injunctions from ideological authorities are extraordinarily far-reaching and exclusionary. They refer to subject matter, attitude and approach, and pertain especially to nationality writings. The common guidelines, which may be quickly verified through scanning Soviet publications, include a number related to ethnic interrelations and more devoted to unification of all groups. Among the first classification are those that assert that literature must strengthen friendship among all ethnic groups of the USSR, or enhance "fraternal cooperation" amongst them. In the second kind appear many that call upon literature to demonstrate that "socialist internationalism" is the sole firm basis for Soviet social intercourse, or that emphasize the emergence of "one new historical community of Soviet people" and its "international unity." Writers are told also to display implacability toward "nationalism," "chauvinism," "national narrow-mindedness," and "nationality conceit," while reflecting devotion to the one Union-wide Communist Party, and to the Soviet homeland as a whole.[4]

Besides guidelines, which are stated frequently and apply broadly to all nationalities, other rules define acceptable premises for literary theory. Among them: primacy must go to what is termed the popular/folk element in the writing; progress is made by moving away from poetry to short prose and on to what is regarded as the ultimate, the full-length prose novel; a proper sequence in literary development must proceed from description to a romantic view of the world, and on to a "realistic" analysis of the human soul and personality. And, in fiction writing, "actuality has preference over literary influence;"

[4] *Natsional'noe i internatsional'noe v literature, fol'klore i iazyke* (Kishinev: Izdatel'stvo "Shtiintsa," 1971); *Unity. Collected Articles on Multi-National Soviet Literature* (Moscow: Progress Publishers, 1975); *Khudozhestvennye iskaniia sovremennoi sovetskoi mnogonatsional'noi literatury* (Kishinev: "Shtiintsa," 1976); *Inqilab wä ädäbiyat* (Tashkent: Ghäfur Ghulam namidägi Ädäbiyat wä Sän'ät Näshriyati, 1977); *Natsional'nyi iazyk i natsional'naia kul'tura* (Moscow: "Nauka," 1978); *Soviet Literature*, 1981, No. 5; and many others.

the material of "life itself" provides the basis for "the principled trend, the writer's outlook" that organizes his artistic creativity.[5]

For Sovnatlit there is yet another tenet requiring respectful acknowledgement from both critics and writers. It originates in the practice of Russian paternalism or tutelage that has faced nationality authors since at least the early 1930s. Though established nationalities already possessed their own strong literary heritage, they have been obliged under the new conditions to defer to Mikhail Y. Lermontov, Leo N. Tolstoy, Anton P. Chekhov, Maxim Gorky and many additional Russian writers as models. Behind this literary paternalism persists the idea that old, civilized groups as well as less cultured nationalities now in the USSR lacked sufficient artistic talent to develop properly by themselves. Most substantial Eastern nationalities had enjoyed some prose writings long before 1920, and many knew the form centuries earlier, though they preferred verse and largely avoided prose. Thus, the notion of Russian superiority that ties itself closely to the writing of prose fiction invents a kind of literary dependence by grafting onto nationality literature a genealogy that is partially artificial.

All these expectations and rules to which authors are subject must condition literary criticism and the writings considerably. It seems plausible to propose that the prescriptions, if closely heeded, would mute, if not strongly stylize, the treatment of nationality awareness in Sovnatlit. In testing this proposition, a formidable problem arises in any attempt to theorize about deciding how much the prescribed treatment of awareness may be regarded as intrinsic and how much extraneous, and how either finding may be evaluated. Assessment of level and quality of writing may help to gain insight into the question.

Because Soviet authors usually belong to the immediate ethnic environment in which they write, most compose for readers able to understand them without translation. Even so, effective writers as artists stand apart figuratively from the people around them, for an author must be in a position to visualize that humanity. The imagina-

[5] K. Zelinskii, "Chto daiut russkoi literature narody SSSR," *Puti razvitiia sovetskoi mnogonatsional'noi literatury* (Moscow: Izdatel'stvo "Nauka," 1967), p. 117 f.; M. Parkhomenko, "The birth of the New Epos," *Unity. Collected Articles . . .*, p. 110.

tive detachment common to good fiction writers esthetically puts them in a posture to determine how dependent on or independent of others' expectations they can remain. But prescriptions inevitably restrict a writer's range of choice by introducing taboos and sanctions that inhibit his communication of true feelings or beliefs in literature, including the normal expression of nationality awareness. In addition, out of pervasive guidance in the field of literature will grow forms especially appropriate to the demands made upon it. In Sovnatlit two varieties of short fiction naturally gained emphasis. One of them, heavy satire, goes far beyond inhibition into the area of intimidation. Slashing satire frequently appeared in Sovnatlit as a menacing means to shape public opinion and reinforce official positions concerning economic, political or social attitudes. An Uzbek author of the Old Soviet school, Abdullah Qahhar (1907-1968), employed this kind of overstatement to attack the standard targets of Marxism: "class enemies," the bourgeoisie, "nationalists," "imperialists," and the like. In one specimen of his invective, "The Healer of the Blind," Mr. Qahhar vehemently assaults Muslim clergy and anti-Soviet guerrillas of an earlier era.[6] True to the form, he makes their ethnic identity and the label of everything in the prose negatively explicit. Not so clearly rendered is the authenticity of the literary tone. Rough satire speaks to a specific audience, for its grotesquery can hardly be appreciated by an unprepared or alien public. Oversimplification like this apparently was meant for undiscriminating children or semi-educated adults.

The other prose form that emerged to prominence under the circumstances was a conventionally-worded didacticism with few pretensions either to high passion or delicate sensitivity. In it, the author customarily illustrates a single line of advice or admonition with a brief episode from everyday life or some minor adventure.

Everywhere among the nationalities, this sort of literature puts great emphasis upon utter devotion to one's duty, for this accords with the commandments in the Communist moral code.[7] The simpler

[6] Abdullah Kahhar, "The Healer of the Blind," *Uzbekistan Speaks. Short Stories* (Moscow: Foreign Languages Publishing House, ca. 1958), pp. 87-115.

[7] "Moral Code of the Builder of Communism," *Program of the Communist Party of the Soviet Union* (New York: International Publishers, 1963), p. 122; Nikita S. Khrushchev, *The Great Mission of Literature and Art* (Moscow: Progress Publishers, 1964), pp. 33-34.

the obligation, seemingly the greater the display in literature of such devotion and the more patronizing the affection shown toward the dutiful person by superiors and author. A Kirgiz or Tajik mailman perseveres through storm, furious artillery fire, injury, or last calls of close personal attachment to deliver private correspondence to farmers or to soldiers. The act is shown to be wholly impersonal, executed in the self-denying manner of religious orders in charitable service. One example:

> They [telegrams] were from the village school's old pupils congratulating the farmers on the new building....'I say, did old Duishen bring these telegrams?' the headmaster asked the lad. 'Yes. He says he whipped his horse all the way to get them here before the meeting closed....'But why is he outside? Tell him to come in'....'He wouldn't come in, he has more mail to deliver, he says'....'Oh, you don't know our Duishen! Duty comes first with him'.[8]

This air of condescension toward a good citizen not only looks down upon the faithful civil servant, it works to depersonalize him into a type. Types of characters warrant their particular literary tones for an entire story, as Duishen has done in this case. The patronizing attitude toward the story's eponym relates intimately to the version of nationality consciousness presented in the fiction. Both the artist narrator and academician epistle writer within the narration come from the same Kirgiz village. But their viewpoint from an unnamed regional center and from Moscow slants backward and downward to that village and the remaining inhabitants, like Duishen, in it. The hamlet where the action occurs, placed on the margin of Kazakh plains and Kirgiz mountains, by its location conveys ethnic

[8] Fatekh Niyazi, "Hurram, the Postman," trans. Rose Prokofieva, *Soviet Literature*, 1981, No. 5, pp.78-87; Chinghis Aitmatov, "Duishen" (written 1961), trans. Olga Shartse, *Tales of the Mountains and Steppes* (Moscow: Progress Publishers, 1969), pp. 86-87.

ambiguity. Consistent with it is a contradictoriness in the personal identity of the principal figure, who, claiming to be the son of a villager long departed from the area, is himself called by the locals: "stranger," "tramp's son and a homeless tramp."[9] Nostalgia for the abandoned rural habitat and life, neither shown to be pleasurable or entirely happy, supplies the dominant tone. "Duishen" also fits into the category of officially encouraged war stories.

These have appeared in numberless versions, sometimes affecting, often slight in form, thin in substance. Such an impersonal tone can be felt in the Azeri story, "The Telegramme," by Elchin (b.1943). An Azeri and a Georgian graduate student, married, lived in a Moscow University dormitory. This post-War generation knows nothing first-hand about its War losses, but, moved by sentiment and a vague sense of guilt, makes a gesture of telegramming one of the deceased back in the Georgian SSR on Soviet VE Day, in a whimsical act of youth.[10] In the course of its light, sporadically lively progress, the flippant tone of this brief tale momentarily allows itself an interpolated rhetorical passage to announce seriously that "May 9th is a testimony to the strength and justice of our fathers and grandfathers. May 9th is also a day of remembering."[11] Thereafter, the tale goes on its programmatic way. By allusions to Uzbek and Daghistanian students it records that Moscow is a cosmopolitan place in which many visit and study but to which their relationship remains that of outsiders.

Otherwise, the Azeri anthology from which this selection came omits almost completely the style of purposive writing exemplified in "The Telegramme." As a group, the stories written after 1945 by authors born since 1925 reveal several things about the matter of ethnic awareness in Azeri and perhaps other Sovnatlit. They focus nearly undeviatingly upon the routines of ordinary life and for the most part on lower middle-class and working people involved in them. Two barbers, elementary teachers, a retired oilfield hand,

[9] Aitmatov, "Duishen," pp. 83, 91, 101.

[10] Mirza Ibragimov, ed., *Azerbaijanian Prose. An Anthology* (Moscow: Progress Publishers, 1977), pp. 344-349.

[11] *Ibid.*, pp.347-348

blacksmiths, a farmer, and the like are the personages. With one or two exceptions, the fiction lacks unusual, interesting ideas or thematic innovation and substance. The literary method and form are consistently conventional, if a confessional piece, probably the least ethnic of the eleven, "The Islands," by Chinghiz Husseinov (b. 1929), is excluded. Despite the kindliness of most personages, and of the storytellers, most of these figures remain remote depictions. The predominant tone surrounding them is melancholy nostalgia verging on grimness. It repeatedly replaces general current engagement and is accompanied with and occasional voicing of slim hope for a good son or a country cottage that will comprise a pleasant future. Noticeable through its absence is any positive allusion to earlier centuries of Azeri life. This omission contributes to the sense of disconnection in the writing and limits the depth that might be helpful. The hiatus adds to the mood of accomplished change, of uneasy contemporaneity.[12]

That air of truncated development, of present time with relation only to limited personal retrospection, communicates Azerbaijanian modernity in one regard quite distinct from the tone in some recent Tajik prose fiction. A special compilation including six stories by different authors born in Tajikistan since 1927 seems to offer more diverse moods. The vigor imparted in their style overcomes any tendency toward sad nostalgia. Simultaneously, they treat tradition strongly and repeatedly within the heart of the plot and esthetics of these works. But, along with these traits, obtrusively sounds a tone like that in some Sovnatlit favored by ideologist in the 1950s. It is a persistent note of patent if homely uplift, present in the work of these six authors. Fazliddin Mukhammadiev's (1928) "The Duel" offers the test of strength between noble and ignoble village wrestlers to teach respect for age, experience, physically-demanding toil, and especially the importance of male dignity and avoidance of envy. Yusuf Akobirov (b. 1937) demonstrates, in his "Hussein-Eightman," the official thesis that happiness is hard, productive manual labor. Sattor Tursun (b. 1946) pointedly shows that the greater demands of a man's artistic handiwork give deeper rewards than more remunerative carving of ordinary utensils. One of Timur Zulfikarov's (b. 1936)

[12] *Ibid.*, pp. 284-371.

eccentric personal versions of Central Asian anecdotes extols the cunning, generosity and resourcefulness of the poor Nasreddin by comparison with a dangerous Manghit tribal governor and his men. Each of these half-dozen authors makes his story demonstrate a moral unambiguously. Though most point it out with undisguised simplicity, the two tales by Zulfikarov, "Quince Dreams" and "Makhmud Talgat-Bek," not only speak with irony but utilize original techniques, material and style. The quality and unmistakable ethnic tone in these last two modern fables composed as folklore, brief and flashing, make a persuasive argument for the affinity between genuine creativity and effective expression of nationality awareness. Zulfikarov, skirting Mukhammadiev's explicitness, dramatizes the peculiar importance of male dignity in Tajik society:

> [Talgat-bek:] 'And do you know me? . . .' . . . [Nasreddin:] 'When you were running and yelling, I did not recognize you, *domullo* [master] . . . But now I see that it's you, our most respected Talgat-bek . . .' [Talgat-bek:] 'You have an evil tongue . . . Like a cobra's tooth . . . You saved me from the cobra and now you're biting me yourself? . . . But I forgive you. You defended me against death, against the albasty [evil one]...'[13]

The governor's quick perception and acknowledgement that youthful Nasreddin had chided him for unmanly fright, haste and demonstrativeness creates the undercurrent giving this entire story its lively color and authentic tone. Mr. Zulfikarov accomplishes his artistic aim with finesse while concurrently satisfying the expectations of official criticism regarding pre-Soviet life. He glorifies the person of the Tajik underdog and denigrates his Uzbek (Manghit) authorities. Only a talented writer could balance the two half-way attractively. At the same time, ethnic identity is artfully complicated by the choice of hero, for Nasreddin Afandi is native to many different nationalities of Central Asia and the outer Middle East. The effectiveness of this

[13] Timur Zulfikarov, "Hoja Nasreddin's First Love. Two Stories from the Book," *Soviet Literature*, 1981, No. 5, p. 128.

treatment depends greatly upon the author's ability to round out the characters, to attribute affirmative qualities of intelligence, wit and gratitude to a villain regularly wholly reviled in Sovantlit. Unlike all-out satire, that attribution successfully risks making the adversary human, and believable.

Mr. Zulfikarov's achievement raises the question of interpreting the anti-intellectualism so noticeable in the writings of various nationalities. Insistence upon treating the activities of very ordinary, unintrospective types became nearly a fetish in Sovnatlit. The single-mindedness made an approach to the clash and clamor of ideas virtually impossible. A conscientious writer could not take the current of thought very far if his hero and milieu imposed limits that barred a reasonable breadth of intellect. The world of simple souls and manual laborers rarely supplies a viewpoint that can represent the exciting play of active minds. Readers of this short fiction get an unreal picture of their group's range and depth, for no normal society lacks intellectual resources and life. No matter how clever the fictive individual, if the writer's sight remains intent upon a character's performance rather than his imagination or choices, literature in this category seldom speaks at length or persuasively about why people behave or think as they do.

The story "Jamila" (1958), by Kirgiz writer Chingiz Aitmatov offers an instance of that studied naive tone. "Jamila" relates a love story about adults mostly through the testimony of a child. The popularity of this uncomplicated tale far beyond the limits of Kirgizistan may be accounted for largely by the author's device of using an innocent young observer to purify an episode from the love affair of the two romantic figures depicted in motion but never thought. For undemanding readers outside Kirgizistan, especially, the appeal lies principally in the writer's deliberate schematization of all his characters and simultaneous confusing of any clear ethnicity. Jamila's lover, Daniyar, becomes a mystical, almost inarticulate Central Asian everyman:

> If I were only able to re-create in some way Daniyar's song! There were hardly any words to it, but without words it revealed a big human heart. Neither before nor after did I ever hear such a song:

> it was neither Kirghiz nor Kazakh, but there was something of both in it. Daniyar had combined the best melodies of the two related peoples and had curiously woven them into a never - to-be-repeated pattern. This was a song of the mountains and steppes, now soaring like the Kirghiz mountains, now vast and rolling like the Kazakh steppes.[14]

By employing the schoolboy narrator, the author somewhat avoids an incongruity sounding in so much fiction from the 1950s. But, the story contained within the rather cumbersome narrative framework retains that troubling immaturity of tone throughout. It, too, works to reduce the ethnic specificity of the composition.

An Uzbek short story form the 1950s demonstrates the function of both the general and the second, interpolated, kind of literary tone already mentioned. "New Year's Party," told almost entirely through dialogue among a few women, starts with household chat and sociability and ends the same way. Interspersed in the piece are fragments that abruptly alter the brittle exchange to make some alien point, in this text, about local politics:

> 'To tell the truth', began Halima, when the door closed behind Vakhijan [husband of a guest], 'auntie is right. Whenever I listen to her I realize that we did not elect her to the district Soviet [council] for nothing. How much longer are we going to stick to our old customs and carry trays of dried fruit and cake every time we visit somebody? It doesn't become us!' [Italics added][15]

The momentary intrusion of that political note into the text of such a story is not the only source of its hortatory tone. The premise

[14] Chingiz Aitmatov, "Jamila," trans. F. Glagoleva, *Tales of the Mountains and Steppes* (Moscow: Progress Publishers, 1969), p. 47.

[15] Rahmat Fayzi, (b. 1918), "New Year's Party," trans. G. Hanna and D. Skvirsky, *Uzbekistan Speaks. Short Stories* (Moscow: Foreign Languages Publishing House, ca. 1958), p. 136; Sa'ida Zunnunova, "The First Step," *ibid.*, pp. 143-153.

motivating this brief work is that traditional customs are harmful and must be cast out. The entire tale adopts the sound of a treatise against old ways and in favor of a modernity symbolized by machines, drinking alcohol in a formerly abstinent Muslim community, and the innovation of social dancing that mixes the sexes.

In a similar vein from the same collection of Uzbek stories comes "The First Step," by Sa'ida Zunnunova (b. 1926), the only post-World War II woman author included in any of the six compilations analyzed here. The girlish tone with which she writes about a woman's emancipation from home, place this work among those illustrating flatly and in the simplest way possible one of the prescribed themes.

An extended counterpart to the interpolated political passages cited earlier may be heard in larger works from the same period. A widely-circulated novella showing this tone consistently from start to finish is the first edition of The Victors (1951), by Sharaf Rashidov (1917-83), former First Secretary of the Communist Party of Uzbekistan and Alternate Member of the Presidium of the Politburo, Central Committee of the Communist Party of the Soviet Union. The novella gives a remarkably impersonal view of farmland and water reclamation work. In tones of an inspirational tract, the work describes a hard rural beginning leading rather suddenly to an idealized conclusion:

> Aikiz and Alimjan walked arm in arm. They came out on the highroad and turned towards the village. There was Altyn-Sai [village] before them, flooded with electricity against which the pale beams of the moon were impotent. The lights radiated in straight, slender lines towards the centre of the village, where they become intricately interwoven. 'Look at all those lights!' Aikiz said. 'How bright they are! It's the light of communism shining on us from tomorrow. Oh, Alimjan-aka, all this happiness is ours!'[16]

[16] Sharaf Rashidov, *The Victors*, trans. Olga Shartse. (Moscow: Foreign Languages Publishing House, ca. 1958), pp. 6-7, 201.

The climax in this final statement means to dramatize a standard theme: humanity's harnessing of the forces of nature. The heroine's penultimate appeal, to the future, rings a note heard persistently in Sovnatlit of the 1950s and earlier. That investment in the life ahead (in a paradise?) harmonizes both the Muslim theology of the traditional culture in Central Asia and the Transcaucasus and the ideological promises of a beautiful future (afterlife?) made in Soviet politics since 1917.

This school of writing from the early post-WWII years comprises a body of literature in which penetration, thought and imagination are ignored unless transmuted into resourcefulness toward practical actions in farming, engineering and comparable occupations. The Sovnatlit corpus of the 1950s thus constitutes the conventions against which subsequent developments in this field must be measured. Given the controls operating in Sovnatlit, the simple esthetic and intellectual level of literature must have been maintained intentionally up to that time. If so, the stature of the writing reveals a good deal about the standards set by publishers who decided to issue the writings. But the sustained, elementary level of most literary performance poses a riddle about Sovnatlit audiences. It would appear that these stories and novellas have been meant either for children or semiliterate adults. Perhaps educated men and women who want fiction are expected to read only long novels. There is a paradox visible in this presumption, for high levels of literacy and education are reported for people of the larger nationalities under the age of 60. Such rigid literary stratification of readers, therefore, now appears so unlikely that a more theoretical explanation may be needed. Sovnatlit may now need to define more surely for itself the audiences for which it should write stories. The works of more recent times that will be reviewed in this discussion still reveal some confusion and ambivalence regarding the purpose and market for literary output. A contemporary Kazakh writer, Olzhas Suleimenov (b. 1936), reminds his readers that the concept of audience is "very fluid and changeable." Simplified writings needed for the 1920s and 1930s, supplied by the Kazakh author Saken Seifullin (1894-1939), among others, have no place in the present literature, for they "no longer 'work' today." Mr. Suleimenov suggests in this way that the deliberately unsophisticated writing that has been provided for nationality readers in the past, and perhaps to some extent still in the present, will fade away as the ideological spokesmen catch up with the public taste:

> Contemporary Soviet writers are more fortunate than their predecessors; nowadays every writer, however complex he may be in his thought, style or manner of writings, has his readers . . . As a social phenomenon, writers are changing less than readers . . . There is a category of writers . . . lagging behind readers in their level of thinking.[17]

That remark may help to account for the survival of weak writers, but it does not quite clarify the motives of government publishing houses that persist in issuing feeble writings. Mr. Suleimenov speaks, too, of carrying on the "universal fight with the lack of talent to expel from man the demon of slavery [dependence?]..." And, in respect to the crucial matter of nationality awareness, he says: "We all want to be both national[ity] and international writers . . ."[18] He sees the challenge of identifying himself both as a Kazakh and a Soviet-wide writer as his duty:

> We are marginal personalities, the products of the interface between at least two cultures; we are simultaneously the bridge between them and the channels of transmission for mutual influence. We represent world culture in our own, and our own in world culture.[19]

The fact that Mr. Suleimenov writes in Russian rather than Kazakh complicates further his testimony that the dual identification of the literary audience, for nationality authors, remains one of the

[17] Olzhas Suleimenov, "We Come to Act," *Soviet Literature*, 1982, No. 6, pp. 156-157.

[18] *Ibid.*, pp.158-159.

[19] *Ibid.*, p. 156.

most basic, unresolved problems facing Sovnatlit. An author must determine not merely how "popular" his level but for whom he writes, primarily - the nationality that gives him sustenance, or the cosmopolis that beckons him beyond it and demands translation or another language of composition. In either choice, the strata within the target audience surely need literary differentiation. How much longer, the Kazakh writer seems to ask, will the authors of his adult fiction have to prepare works accessible to the children and childlike of their own nationality? Without equivocation, he declares his personal preference of audience to be the intellectual élite of his Kazakh nationality.[20]

Choosing an audience will help to move an author out of ambivalence over his readership. To realize his aims takes much more than the writer's initial decision. In attempting to create the fictional characters he wishes, a major accomplishment is to endow them with believable traits and permit them appropriate behavior, whether positive or negative. This achievement has been elusive. In the Soviet East and elsewhere among Soviet nationalities, the topic of presenting persuasive "heroes" in the writing has only recently, as a decade earlier, received special attention from literary managers and official critics. The editor of the widely-circulated (some 200,000 copies monthly) Uzbek-language literary journal, Shärq yulduzi, wrote in early 1982 that Uzbek writers were still facing difficulty in drawing personages with plausible ethnic identity:

> . . . one further defect in creating the images of our contemporaries is revealed in delineating their internationalist and nationalist (milliylik) aspects. Some of our heroes may be well shown as internationalists, but they have been wrenched from the nationality (milliy) soil. They are rendered in a form devoid of nationality particularities. However, various of our literati overwhelm their heroes with nationality particularities. In imbuing them with the spirit of internationalism they stumble badly. Both limitations do harm to creation of the full-blooded,

[20] *Ibid.*, p. 156.

> firm image of our contemporary person, and hamper the flourishing of our literature.[21]

The reemphasis upon "positive heroes" is meant to persuade writers to put before the eyes of impressionable readers personages who can serve as acceptable models. Characterization is an important consideration, but the effect of stressing only one facet of fiction writing probably will be piecemeal, at best. Nonetheless, the Uzbek editor relays a valuable perception when he notices that the literature of his nationality and others has been constrained in communicating the ethnic identity of the groups convincingly.

In this regard, short fiction published in the 1970s and 1980s seems to differ significantly from stories and novellas circulated in the late 1940s and 1950s. To begin with, quite a few stories in the recently published collections are unable to refrain from some moralizing, thus emulating what came before. But now, they both minimize the programmatic comment and the blatant illustration of prescribed themes so prominent in earlier writing. Most valuable, they generally testify to greater command than before of techniques used in modern prose writing. These changes make generalizing about the effectiveness of Sovnatlit in communicating an awareness of nationality identity more exacting. Periodization must be sensitive to the development throughout even short periods.

In selections from seventeen Kazakh male authors published as an anthology very recently, the difference between much of the fiction by the writers born before 1930 and writing from younger men makes the point strongly. One early example, "The Grey Stork," (1959), by Takhavi Akhtanov (b. 1923), typifies the category of didactic works promoting approved themes. Here, "friendship between ethnic groups" mixes Ukrainian and Kazakh young people. Again, the story treats the routine life of rural villagers and farmers, spiced by the presence of one exotic outsider. The stiff tone of committee-meeting dialogue already familiar from some Tajik and Uzbek writings of the early period can be heard here as well.[22] By contrast, in the same

[21] Hafiz Äbdusämätaw, "KPSS XXVI s"ezdi wä qähräman mäsäläsi. Dairä stal ätrafidä suhbät," *Shärq yulduzi*, 1982, No. 1, p. 158.

[22] Takhavi Akhtanov, "The Grey Stork," *The Voice of the Steppe. Modern Kazakh Short Stories* (Moscow: Progress Publishers, 1981), pp.138-139.

compilation of tales, Dukenbai Doszhanov (b. 1942) conveys an elegy to Kazakh folk life in his story "Kumys" (1974). And Mukhtar Magauin (b. 1940), like Doszhanov from a rural family, in "An Archival Story" skillfully dramatizes some moral and intellectual dilemmas that face rising young Kazakh scholars as they compete for position and fame. Sherkhan Murtzaev (b. 1932), less smoothly but nevertheless with effect captures, in his brief story, "Song of the Cicada," the touching strength of loving memory aroused by an almost laughably inept and anachronistic montage. An itinerant photographer has prepared it for a woman who never before possessed a picture of herself together with her husband, a war casualty. Rollan Seisenbaev (b. 1946) offers the most urban, modern of these tales in his short "Saturday is over..." (1977). Consistent with time and setting, its young people exhibit no visible or hypothetical roots in the culture of any specific nationality. Jaunty tone and lively style suit the subject well. Both accord with the frivolity of the developing flirtation and the total lack of significance, in these scenes, of any identity other than youthfulness. Mr. Seisenbaev succeeds in reproducing the kind of instant, complete communication possible only to members of the same nationality and generation.

Like "Saturday is over...," another pleasant story published elsewhere by the Kazakh writer Sain Muratbekov (b. 1936) is remarkable for its lack of underlying guilt or sense of externally motivated duty, hallmarks of the 1950s. Mr. Muratbekov's "Kamen's Forest" nicely epitomizes in the central figure, Kamen, a pudgy, happy farmer, the growth in fictional attitude that has been occurring in Sovnatlit. This unheroic man's joy in tree planting and procreation - his children and many others swarm around him when he romps with them - and his likeable consistency of behavior and amiable temperament remove from this fiction absolutely any suspicion of inspired theme. This holds true in spite of the fact that the story treats two constant topics of Soviet literary prescription: the joy of labor and the ordinary person's innate goodness. Effective writing and the author's point of view have given the story a tone of natural authenticity rarely achieved in previous short prose by nationality writers.[23] "Kamen's

[23] Sain Muratbekov, "Kamen's Forest," *Soviet Literature*, 1982, No. 12, pp. 77-84.

Forest" appears in the same collection with a number of other newer stories, by Chingiz Aitmatov, the Kirgiz writer, by Maksud Ibraghimbekov (b. 1935), an Azeri, by Tashli Kurbanov (b. 1934), a Turkmen, and others. They maintain the focus upon human behavior in private family life. Tensions between husband and wife, children's affection, giving and receiving love, heartbreak and heartburn take up the foreground of these stories. Of necessity, the earlier preoccupations with ideology and compulsory performance of duty are shifted to the background. Just as empty of insistent moralizing and pangs of conscience are stories heavy with anthropomorphism appearing in this same compilation and in others by Timur Pulatov (b. 1939), an Uzbek, and colleagues from various nationalities. They write about yaks vs. a dishonest veterinarian, horses, a homesick camel, and other creatures from the animal kingdom. A similar nature tale published in yet another collection of recent Uzbek literature follows the life of an imperious old, soaring kite. Despite the unhuman protagonist, the bird counsels by its action all who would live a satisfying, stable existence: husband your strength for the long pull and avoid overstepping the boundaries of custom.[24]

Most short fiction by the writers born at least since 1925 in this group repeats patterns observed among the other nationalities. These Uzbek stories explore human feelings and traits. Utkir Khashimov (b. 1941), in "Happiness," shows his heroine's tolerance, generosity and patience in a search for a kind of happiness at once diffuse, elusive, but living within her, if anywhere. Ulmas Umarbekov (b. 1934), in "Golden Leaves," meditates on natural beauty, cleansing rainfall, and some parallels in natural and human dynamics. Pirimkul Kadyrov (b. 1928) writes in "Hope" about catharsis through removal of uncertainty and the release of feeling among members of a family when expected bad news arrives. And Maksud Kariev (b. 1926) evokes in his brief paean, "Moon Magic," to the mystery of youthful bliss under a spring moon, the hint of loss. He links them delicately to the equally marvelous influence for good exerted by a terribly ill wife who, through her unfailing capacity to give and accept love, brings out the best in everyone around her. A laconic mention of

[24] Timur Pulatov, "The Lord of the Territory," *Soviet Literature*, 1982, No. 3, pp. 109-124.

political and occupational work yet to be completed by the narrator places both topics well on the periphery of the story.[25]

The soberness and depth in each of those Uzbek stories contrasts noticeably with the happier Kazakh selection already surveyed. That somber mood is matched by the dark tone of several other writings that have recently appeared in the Uzbek-language literary press. Äbdulqasim Mämäräsulaw's "The Traveler" follows the excruciating downward trail of a drunken ex-convict whose destiny is made depressingly clear by his own behavior within the first hours of his release from a substantial prison term.[26] In "The Report," by Mämätqul Häzrätqulaw, a hardworking farm foreman's shocking encounter with his farm's dishonest head manager (chairman) leaves troubling moral questions alive at the end.[27] Yet, for Sovnatlit, Ubäydullä Sadiqaw may have written the most unusual of these four stories. His "Strangers" depicts severe psychological alienation in a young Uzbek woman. This disturbing account alludes with restraint to ethnic identity by reference to a little-known place name, not one of the historic cities, and by casual mention of the sound of language. A registrar in the bureau of vital statistics speaks "with a Tatar accent." A blonde, unfriendly Russian encountered during the mountain hike understands no Uzbek. These allusions establish the nationality of the characters without ever saying the word "Uzbek."

The tone in this story derives not wholly from the main "stranger," who consistently shows frightened anxiety. Though comfortably living in town, and before long married to a professor, this "village girl" longs, not for her hamlet and her divorced parents but for a life in the wild, and away from people. Her husband's closing oberservation that she has changed and his advice that she must seek a good psychiatrist for help fills her with searing pain and leaves her, as usual, mute. These feelings, expressed most frequently by tears, are known to the reader only through the intervention of the omnipresent

[25] Maksud Kariev, "Moon Magic," *Soviet Literature*, 1982, No. 3, pp. 125-136.

[26] Äbdulqasim Mämäräsulaw, "Yolawchi," *Shärq yulduzi*, 1982, No. 1, pp. 144-152.

[27] Mämätqul Häzrätqulaw, "Räpart," *Shärq yulduzi*, 1982, No. 2, pp. 89-93.

author. Otherwise, the tone remains surprisingly detached, clinically descriptive, because the aloof scholar is in his way also a stranger. A fourth melancholy Uzbek tale, "The Unworn Ring" (1970-1981), by Aqiljan Husänaw (b. 1932), balances the two about men, just cited, with another treatment, unmelodramatic, of orphaned women in despair,[28] one of whom resentfully lapses into the status of a qäri qiz (old maid) for whom the usual Uzbek system of arranging marriages has failed.

If newer short stories by authors from among the nationalities were to precede along the lines marked out by these specimens of very recent Uzbek fiction, it would be obvious that a literary change had taken place. Critics would have firm ground for pointing both to an altering over time and to differences between nationalities in writing this one genre. For all its diversity in form and subject, the imaginative prose of well-established nationalities in the USSR seems to emit some recognizable literary tones. These are evidently linked to a definite period, to mood and use of a specific genre, and perhaps to a certain nationality. Among those tones, one in particular usually dominates a coherent period, such as the fairly self-reliant 1970s and 1980s so far. If one sound distinguishes the expression of a given nationality in the country at a certain time, literary tone may in that sense offer a clue to identifying the awareness of nationality conveyed in contemporary Sovnatlit. Azeri, Kazakh, Tajik and Uzbek short fiction of the 1970s and 1980s has been seen to exhibit such differences among its branches, even though those geographically proximate nationalities have many cultural traits in common. Moreover, the dominant tones permeating that and most other nationality literature will probably not be duplicated exactly in Russian writings, owing to their separate intellectual history and tutelary status.

An author creates literary tone mainly by communicating in writing a certain attitude toward or relationship with the material of the story. The examples given above show that the writer can generate tone through revealing, however inexplicitly, his or her own view of the audience for whom the work may be meant. An author will find his or her individual tone when the internal voice in all the work

[28] Ubäydullä Sadiqaw, "Beganälär," *Shärq yulduzi*, 1982, No. 2, pp. 94-103; Aqiljan Husänaw, "Täqilmägän uzuk," *ibid.*, pp. 74-82.

created during a significant stage of esthetic development begins to speak perceptibly to the reader not necessarily forever in a monotone but in related keys and manner. The predominate tone conveyed by a story in turn governs those more temporary frames of mind or moods displayed in the literature through situation, characterization, diction and verbal devices. Broadly, measuring these intangibles as components in the expression of nationality consciousness entails applying to them a range of relative correspondences stretching between what may be considered most intrinsic to a well-developed nationality's literature and what seems most extrinsic. The authentic hum or song of a given nationality literature arises from writers' sure use of native, mature idiom and subject. An identifying tone of nationality emanates from writing when numbers of the group's authors consistently achieve a particular indigenous tone among them at about the same period. Amateur, mediocre authors probably have no inkling of the importance or effect of genuine literary tone. Achieving believable, appropriate tone seems to relate closely to a higher level and quality of writing rather than a lower one. Adult Sovnatlit that consistently displays a naive approach to any serious subject inescapably emits a false tone. That childlike outlook on life of a full-grown character alerts the reader to an author's condition or attitude of tutelage. Generalized tutelage in a work connotes a relationship of dependence for author, audience, or both. The reverse of independence in literature indicates the presence of an inadequate sense of discrete nationality.

Well-written stories impart an overall intonation that appears to transmit a crucial identifier (speak the same language) between author and audience. The greater the coincidence between the attitude and resulting tone of the author and readers, the wider the writer's nationality audience may become. In addition, to that broader tone, another, special voice noticeable in post-World War II fiction ordinarily served briefly and intermittently within compositions to set off passages intended to act as strong reminders to the public of right thinking or orthodox ideological belief. This second classification of literary tone nearly always breaks the unity of the single work by drawing the reader's attention away from the main narration. Interpolated tone attracts notice by its often reverent, righteous or indignant pitch. Quickly perceptible in a story, the intervening tone invariably, no doubt purposely, sounds at least slightly out of tune within its immediate context. It often repeats formulas, stock phrases or paraphrased slogans, thus momentarily shifting the writing style. This technique customarily proves to typify fiction published by the older, more political authors. But, under exceptional circumstances, that tone can be indifferent to age, impersonal and unindividual, occasionally scattered among nationality writings from different times. In the stories from the last two decades, it seems an anachronism. In any period, such passages expose by contrast the basic literary tone of a composition.

Of all the logical possibilities available to writers, one, a persistent absence of gentle irony, may typify, as much as any other single defining factor, the literary tone noticeable in the imaginative prose selected from Sovnatlit. Light irony, widespread in late twentieth-century literary outlook, seemingly has been excluded from Sovnatlit by the prevalence of a specifically countervailing tone. The antipodes of subtle literary irony theoretically may be multiple and difficult to isolate. But, in Sovnatlit, only one or two probably can be pertinent. Crude sarcasm and Juvenalian satire excoriate their target, deafening the sensitive ear. At another extreme, the indicativeness or positivism prevailing earlier in much Sovnatlit, and still somewhat alive, cannot be accounted a random choice by authors. It emerges naturally from the facts of Soviet life, essentially reflecting the high degree of guidance, expectation and prescription exercised in managing Sovnatlit.

Un-ironic writing, our literary examples show, may lay exclusive claim to few modes of expression other than those that are declarative. Quiet irony joins compatibly with humor, tragedy, even sober realism. It combines well with them to add nuance to the communication of feeling. This restrained irony cannot so easily, if at all, harmonize with fervent utterances of faith or true belief, with heated moralizing or convinced utopianism. Those are styles with which subdued ambiguity, intellectual playfulness, or complex human duality are at odds. Programmatic Sovnatlit, too, appears to stifle overtones and to negate unorthodox symbolism. Not surprisingly, the more programmatic the literature, the less ironically it speaks to an audience unaccustomed to reading between the lines. The general incidence of unsatiric writing that lacks the tone of irony may help explain the diffuseness of nationality awareness in some Sovnatlit.

But, into the newest versions of it are slipping a few shades of irony. This equips authors with finer tools than they used earlier for the intricacies of transmitting group awareness. That is timely, because, especially in the East, an unprecedented series of young generations, educated and extraordinarily numerous, is now rapidly filling these very societies. The perceptive nationality author writing about contemporary life will condense for them what only someone like himself knows with intimate familiarity about his people and generation. No introduction of conventional signs of nationality will be wanted by these young readers. Nor will the up-to-date storyteller rely upon the traditional signals. Internal to each nationality, the literary tone that reaches this growing audience will be comprised of that right configuration of values taken in the priority uniquely associated, in their own perception, with the Azeri, Kazakh, Kirgiz, Tajik or Uzbek imagination. Today's better authors compress nationality consciousness into the whole texture and depth of their brief works.

The best published new stories now appearing have not somehow evaded control and prescription. They result from the qualitative improvement of the writers in their craft as well as from increasing opportunities for publishing unusual works that go beyond the conformities of the past. The newer writers mostly abjure even implicit but instantly defining comparisons of their nationality with other ethnic groups. That makes expressing the distinctions between nationalities of this kind more elusive, less open than ever, quite aside from the constraints placed upon the process by ideology. In the end, today's literature conforms with the earlier writings in one sphere vital to this analysis of nationality identity in fiction. Soviet taboos enforced in prescriptive criticism still block the searching exploration of ethnic interrelation portrayed in much of world literature. This tendency in the USSR greatly limits the expression of nationality life in literature. By denying the lively ethnic current crackling in everyday Soviet sayings, jokes, slurs and behavior, Sovnatlit continues to offer its readers a stylized, unrealistic picture of the external aspects of nationality identity among and between the Soviet Union's ethnic groups.

What do those contradictory imperatives - new flexibility vs. old dogmatism - mean for Central Asia in the future? Sovnatlit, because of its idealizing purpose, cannot fully mirror present-day ethnic attitudes on its pages. Until prohibitions embodied in the slogan "friendship between ethnic groups" (*khălqlăr dostlighi*; *dŭstii khălqha*) become neutralized by public indifference or official reinterpretation, ethnic candor will not surface from the literary underworld, except perhaps in samizdat; therefore, current literature represents public life rather directly. The ethnic hypocrisy that has been built into the value system conditions much of the contemporary creative writing. At best, the new prose supplies subtle echoes of the realities in daily life and avoids the falsity of ethnic stereotyping.

Barring regression into doctrinaire socialist realism, Central Asian short fiction can be expected to move further toward greater esthetic accomplishment in the next decades. That tendency should enhance ethnic expressiveness for each Central Asian nationality as well, perhaps, as for Central Asia as a whole. It can likewise reinforce genuine ethnic group self-awareness by articulating the idiom and helping to ward off cultural denial or assimilation.

A NEGLECTED SOURCE ON CENTRAL ASIAN HISTORY:

THE 17TH-CENTURY YASAVĪ HAGIOGRAPHY

MANĀQIB AL-AKHYĀR

Devin DeWeese

Western students of Central Asia are often hampered in their work by the difficulty of arranging access to historical sources preserved only in manuscript collections and archives in the republics of the former Soviet Union. While it is hoped that, with independence, the academic communities in the Central Asian republics will increase the accessibility of their manuscript heritage to the level prevailing in most of the world, it is worth noting that here and there outside Central Asia we may find untapped but rich and rewarding sources on Central Asian history which have long been accessible but have nevertheless been all but ignored. Such is the case with the work which is the subject of this brief report, a 17th-century hagiographical account of a Khorezmian saint: although one copy of this work was catalogued nearly a century ago, with a description which ought to have drawn the attention of specialists on Central Asian history and religion, it has to my knowledge never been examined or cited as a source for the history of Central Asian Sufism.

The work in question is the *Manāqib al-akhyār*, completed in 1036/1626 by a certain Muḥammad Qāsim, known by the *takhalluṣ* "Riżvān;" it is an account of the life and sayings of the author's father, Sayyid Jamāl ad-Dīn of Khorezm, known as "Khoja Dīvānah Sayyid Atā'ī," who died in 1016/1607. It is not certain where the work was written, since the subject of the biography spent at least part of his life in India and died there in the company of his sons and followers; we have no subsequent information on the work's author, nor do we know if he returned to Central Asia. In any case, the work is, I believe, an important source on the history of Central Asia in the post-Mongol era, and is especially invaluable as an example of hagiographical literature produced within Sufi circles affiliated with the Yasavī order; in particular, it illustrates an interesting pattern of interaction between the Naqshbandī and Yasavī *ṭarīqah*s, reflecting on the one hand an apparent attempt to assert the independence and integrity of the Yasavīyah in terms of praxis, and on the other hand betraying Naqshbandī dominance by "imitating" the latter order in doctrinal and hagiographical presentation. It is clearly worthy of further study, and the brief description here is intended only to (re-)introduce the work to students of Central Asia.

In the first volume of the catalogue of Persian manuscripts in the India Office Library in London, published in 1903, Hermann Ethé provided a good description of what is still the only copy of this work registered in a published catalogue;[1] his treatment is marred only by the title he assigned the work. The India Office copy is incomplete at the end, and although the correct title is mentioned just before the text in this manuscript breaks off, it is not immediately apparent that this is indeed the title of the work. Ethé thus referred to it by the generic designation *Maqāmāt-i Sayyid Atāʾī*. On the basis of Ethé's description, the work was accorded a brief mention, under that title, in the section on biographies in C. A. Storey's survey of Persian literature,[2] but outside these two reference works, this Central Asian hagiography has evidently drawn no attention. My own study of the work began in 1983,[3] on the basis of a microfilm of the India Office copy, which I examined more closely several years later while preparing a conference paper.

In July, 1988, during a research trip to manuscript collections throughout India, I worked briefly at the Raza Library in Rampur.[4] While six volumes of the catalogue of this library's Arabic manuscripts have been published, the Persian collection remains virtually unknown, described as it is only in a topically-arranged handlist in two large volumes. As I checked through this handlist, I found mention, in the section on *tadhkirahs*,[5] of a work with the unfamiliar title

[1] *Catalogue of the Persian Manuscripts in the Library of the India Office*, I (Oxford, 1903), cols. 268-270, No. 644.

[2] *Persian Literature: A Bio-bibliographical Survey*, I/2 (London, 1953), p. 987, No. 1315.

[3] See my "Atāʾīya Order," *Encyclopaedia Iranica*, vol. 2, pp. 904-905.

[4] I would like to express my gratitude to the Raza Library's officiating director, Akbar Ali Khan Arshizadah, for his extraordinary kindness and hospitality in facilitating my work in Rampur.

[5] Imtiyāz ʿAlī ʿArshī, ed., *Fihrist-i makhṭūṭāt-i fārsī*, vol. 2, pp. 123-171.

Manāqib al-akhyār, ascribed to "Muḥammad Qāsim b. Khoja Dīvānah Atā'ī Ḥusaynī with the *takhalluṣ* "Riżvān"," and listed as having been completed in 1036 A.H.; inspection of the manuscript itself[6] revealed that the work it contained was identical with the work I had known from the India Office copy. The Rampur copy is complete, and confirms how nearly complete the India Office copy is: in all 27 1/2 lines preserved in the Rampur copy are missing from the India Office manuscript,[7] but these lines are nevertheless important for clearly establishing the correct title of the work as *Manāqib al-akhyār*, a chronogram for 1036 A.H., the year it was completed.

The India Office manuscript runs to 126 folios of 15 lines each; the Rampur manuscript's 147 folios also run to 15 lines each, with narrower columns accounting for its greater length. Both copies were written in a medium-sized *nastaʿlīq*. The Rampur manuscript is more carefully written than the India Office copy, but appears to be somewhat more recent; neither manuscript is dated, nor is there any indication as to where each copy was completed. The fact that both manuscripts were preserved in Indian collections suggests that they were copied in the subcontinent, and may further reinforce the supposition that the work was written in India rather than in Central Asia. Without a clearer identification of the author, however, we cannot insist that his father's memory was wholly "transferred" to India.

The work begins with a brief preface (IO ff. 1b-6b, Raza ff. 1b-7a) on the reason for its composition; it was intended, the author writes, as an abbreviation of two earlier works (neither of which appears to have survived) by two disciples of Sayyid Jamāl ad-Dīn, namely Ākhūnd Mawlānā Darvīsh Tāshkandī and Qāżī Jān Muḥammad b. Qāżī Khān Bukhārī, and was compiled at the urging of the author's elder brother, Khoja Abū'l-Ḥasan. The preface closes with an outline of the disposition of the work, which is divided into a *muqaddimah*, four *maqāms*, and a *khātimah*.

The *muqaddimah* (IO ff. 6b-14b, Raza ff. 7a-18a) is a brief discussion of the meaning of sainthood, the classes of saints, and the

[6] The copy is registered under the designation *Tadhkirah* No. 2378, but the designation "*Suluk Fārsī* No. 724" appears on the manuscript itself.

[7] The last words in the India Office copy appear on l. 5 of fo. 146b of the Rampur manuscript, in which the work ends on l. 2 of f. 147b.

proofs and classifications of miracles. Several definitions of sainthood (*vilāyat*) are given, citing the works of early Sufis such as Hujvīrī, Abū Yazīd Bisṭāmī and Abū Ṭālib al-Makkī as well as those of 14th- and 15th-century figures such as Jalāl ad-Dīn Davvānī and Abū ʿAlī Jurjānī. It is significant that in discussing the two classes of saints the author clearly shows his preference for what may be termed Naqshbandī-style sanctity; the *ʿuzlatīyān*, those who seek seclusion and avoid social contact, are for him clearly inferior to the *ʿishratīyān*, "who see unity in multiplicity" and therefore participate in normal social interaction. Even the famous Naqshbandī dictum of *khalvat dar anjuman* ("solitude in the crowd") is cited as a virtue of the latter class of saints, an indication of the dominance of the Naqshbandīyah in defining Sufi doctrinal discourse in Central Asia by the time this work was written.

Further discussion of saints and sainthood focuses on the famous Sufi teaching of the *quṭb*, the spiritual "Axis" of each age, and the esoteric hierarchy of his supporters (i.e. the four *awtād*, the seven *abrār*, the 40 *abdāl*, etc.); a brief exposition of types of "miracles" (e.g. the prophetic *muʿjizah* and the *karāmāt* of the saints) closes the introduction. It is again instructive that among the works cited on the issue of miracles is the *Faṣl al-khiṭāb* of Khoja Muḥammad Pārsā - again, a Naqshbandī work, arguably the most influential and widely cited Sufi work of Central Asia, whose prominence attests to the intellectual vitality of the Naqshbandīyah and its consequent penetration of other *ṭariqahs*. No works of Yasavī figures are cited, and this pattern holds true throughout the *Manāqib al-akhyār*: even when sayings of Khoja Aḥmad Yasavī himself are recorded (which is quite rarely), they are clearly drawn from Naqshbandī literary traditions (such as the biographies of Bahāʾ ad-Dīn Naqshband or the well-known *Rashaḥāt-i ʿayn al-ḥayāt*). Aside from the two lost biographies of Sayyid Jamāl ad-Dīn cited in the preface, no Yasavī hagiography or doctrinal work is referred to in the text.

The first *maqām* (IO ff. 14b-30b, Raza ff. 18a-38b) is perhaps the most important section of the work from a historical and biographical perspective; it is devoted to the spiritual and natural lineage of Sayyid Jamāl ad-Dīn, and thus includes invaluable material on the earlier figures of the Yasavī order. Here we learn that the Sayyid's birthplace was the *vilāyat-i Khwārazm va Khīvaq*, called "the place of origin of the people of God and the source of the lights of the Absolute" (*maṭlaᶜ-i mardān-i ḥaqq va manbaᶜ-i anvār-i muṭlaq*), and that his lineage went back to "Ḥaẓrat-i Quṭb al-Hudā, Sayyid Atā," who was among the great *shaykh*s of the Turks.[8]

Sayyid Jamāl ad-Dīn's father was named Sayyid Pādshāh Khoja "Pardah-pūsh," who served as spiritual guide in his region in the "*silsilah-i jahrīyah-i yasavīyah.*" When Sayyid Jamāl ad-Dīn was four months old, the account continues, the "*fitnah*" of Shah Ismāᶜīl took place; this allows us to date his birth to the year 916/1510-11, when Ṣafavid troops occupied Khorezm following the defeat of Muḥammad Shībānī Khan. Sayyid Pādshāh Khoja was martyred during these disorders, and his son was left in the care of a certain Khoja Bābā, a *murīd* of the father; this figure and his influence are dealt with later in the work, which now turns to tracing the natural lineage of Sayyid Jamāl ad-Dīn - and in this case his natural lineage corresponds to his Yasavī *silsilah* as well.

Sayyid Pādshāh Khoja was the son and pupil of Sayyid Ismāᶜīl Khoja, who was in turn the son and pupil of Sayyid Quraysh Khoja; the latter's father and spiritual guide was Sayyid Vilāyat Khoja, who was trained by his father Sayyid ᶜAbdullāh, known as "Zarbakhshī" as a result of his miraculous transformation of a stone into gold. It is with regard to this latter figure's father, the "founder" of this branch of the Yasavīyah - Sayyid Ata himself - that we find some of the most important details provided by the present work. After noting that Sayyid Ata's name was Sayyid Aḥmad and that he was a contemporary and associate of the eminent Khojagānī shaykh Khoja ᶜAlī ᶜAzīzān Rāmitanī (d. 736/1336), the work describes the entry of Sayyid Ata and his three companions - Uzun Ḥasan Ata, Ṣadr Ata, and Badr Ata - into the service of Zangī Ata of Tashkent; Zangī Ata was the disciple of Ḥakīm Ata, who was in turn a disciple of Ahmad Yasavī himself. The account here is clearly based on that of the well-known Naqshbandī hagiographical work of the early 16th century, the *Rashaḥāt-i ᶜayn al-ḥayāt*, which is in fact cited, but the subsequent

[8] The author is careful to note that there are three groups of *sayyids* in "Tūrān" known for the soundness of their lineages: the sayyids of Tirmidh, the "*sādāt-i Sayyid Atāʾī*," and the sayyids of Mīr Ḥaydar (who, he says, are in fact related by marriage to the "Sayyid Atāʾī" sayyids).

career of Sayyid Ata is covered much more extensively in the present work than in any other hagiographical source.

Following their mystical training under Zangī Ata, the four companions were sent off by their *shaykh*, with Sayyid Ata going to the Dasht-i Qipchāq and to "the farthest reaches of the Manghït and Tatar;" there, through wonders and miracles, he led "most of the Uzbek khans" (*akthar az khānān-i uzbakīyah*), who were still infidels, to the felicity of Islam.[9] "Many groups among the *ulūsāt-i uzbak va tātār*" accepted Islam through his efforts, and day by day the religion of Islam grew stronger, until "in the steppes of those regions the sound of prayer and the summons to prayer replaced the voice of the [pagan] bard" (*be-jā-yi āvāz-i ōẕān bāng-i namāz-u-aẕān baland kardīd*, IO f. 16b, Raza f. 20b).

More importantly, perhaps, the author goes on to stress the close relationship established between the khans of the Uzbeks and Sayyid Ata's family as a result of Sayyid Ata's purported role as "spiritual guide" to the Uzbeks; he notes the establishment of kinship ties through marriage, and the evidently important political and ceremonial role assigned to Sayyid Ata's descendants at the feasts and councils of the Uzbeks.[10] As a result, the author writes, "This *ṭarīqah* has been strong from the time of the holy Sayyid Ata down to the present." Interestingly, however, the author alludes to the growing competition for influence and prestige at court from unspecified "groups," by which term Naqshbandī Sufi communities are clearly intended; here we are no doubt justified in finding yet another reflection of the ongoing rivalry between Yasavī and Naqshbandī communities.

Following a final well-known anecdote about Sayyid Ata, cited from the *Maqāmāt* of Bahā' ad-Dīn Naqshband (i.e. the *Anīs aṭ-ṭālibīn*), the author tells us that Sayyid Ata died in Khorezm and was buried there, and that his grave was still in his time a pilgrimage center (*maṭāf-i ikhlāṣ-mandān-i jihān-ast*) over which horsetail standards

[9] This passage most likely echoes popular tales still current about the role of Sayyid Ata in converting to Islam the Khan Özbek of the Golden Horde.

[10] I have discussed this issue, with reference to the *Manāqib al-akhyār* and other sources, in a forthcoming article, "The Descendants of Sayyid Ata and the Rank of *Naqīb* in Central Asia."

(*parcham-hā-yi tūgh*) were erected. He then offers further particulars about the Khorezmian descendants of Sayyid Ata, mentioning a Sayyid ʿUthmān (who is known also from an 18th-century Khivan hagiography, the *Tadhkirah-i Ṭāhir Īshān*[11]) and a Sayyid Ḥusām ad-Dīn; the latter figure must be identified with the Sayyid Ḥusām ad-Dīn Qatāl known from Abū'l-Ghāzī as a descendant of Sayyid Ata who was instrumental in the expulsion of Qïzïlbash troops from Khorezm and the "conquest" of that country by the Uzbeks under Ilbars and Balbars.[12] The present text provides no confirmation of the specific events portrayed by Abū'l-Ghāzī, but does stress the popularity of Sayyid Ḥusām ad-Dīn and the large numbers of "great and small" among the *pādshāh*s and their troops who sought the initiatory *bayʿat* from him. He also mentions the attachment of the *sayyid*s of Sayyid Ata's lineage to the vocal *dhikr* (using both the terms *dhikr-i jahrī* and *dhikr-i arrah*), and again notes the coincidence of spiritual and natural lineage from Sayyid Ata down to Sayyid Pādshāh Khoja "Pardah-pūsh."

The balance of the first *maqām* is devoted to the spiritual links between Sayyid Jamāl ad-Dīn and the major Central Asian orders, beginning naturally with the Yasavīyah/Jahrīyah. Here the Yasavī *silsilah* is again traced back from Sayyid Ata to Zangī Ata, and then to Ḥakīm Ata and finally to Khoja Aḥmad Yasavī and his two primary *shaykh*s, Arslan Baba and the famous Yūsuf Hamadānī. Most of the account is drawn from the *Rashaḥāt*, but in several cases the author clearly must have drawn upon unspecified written sources which have not survived (perhaps the two earlier biographies of Sayyid Jamāl ad-Dīn) or upon oral tradition preserved within the Yasavī *ṭarīqah*.

The author briefly alludes to Sayyid Jamāl ad-Dīn's links with the Kubravīyah, offering no names or details, before turning to his place in the Naqshbandī *silsilah*. Sayyid Jamāl ad-Dīn's connection to the latter order is through "Khoja Bābā," mentioned earlier, who cared for the orphaned Sayyid following his father's martyrdom, and this

[11] MS Tashkent, Institute of Oriental Studies of the Academy of Sciences of Uzbekistan, Inv. No. 855, ff. 67a-67b.

[12] Cf. P. I. Desmaisons, ed. and tr., *Histoire des Mongols et des Tatares par Aboul-Ghâzî Béhâdour Khan* (St. Petersburg, 1871-74; repr. Amsterdam, 1970), text pp. 196-197, tr. pp. 211-212.

figure's life is now related. He was called Khoja Abū'l-Ḥasan, was also from the lineage of Sayyid Ata (though in what branch is not related), and was also a native of Khorezm. He was, we are told, originally in the service of Sayyid Pādshāh Khoja, but with his *shaykh*'s permission left Khorezm, together with his younger brother Sayyid Muḥammad, and entered the service of the eminent Naqshbandī shaykh Khoja ʿUbaydullāh Aḥrār in the "*vilāyat-i Māwarā'n-nahr va Shāsh*;" from the latter expression it is not clear at which stage of Khoja Aḥrār's career (i.e. in Tashkent or in Samarqand) the Khorezmian *sayyids* must have served him. Both brothers, we learn, received the *bayʿat* from Khoja Aḥrār and reached an exalted level of mystical attainment, whereupon Khoja Aḥrār ordered them to return to Sayyid Pādshāh Khoja in Khorezm. They did so, but while Sayyid Muḥammad Khoja occupied himself with the training of *murīds* in "one of the towns of Khorezm," Khoja Bābā sought permission for a period of seclusion in the desert; this was granted, and Khoja Bābā pursued this vocation until the calamity of Shah Ismāʿīl and Sayyid Pādshāh Khoja's martyrdom, when he took over the training of his master's son, Sayyid Jamāl ad-Dīn.

The account then turns to the Naqshbandī *silsilah* from Khoja Aḥrār back, citing interesting details on each link and pointing out the origin of the division between the *silsilah-i khafīyah* and the *silsilah-i jahrīyah* in the choice of silent vs. vocal *dhikr* made by Khoja ʿAbd al-Khāliq Ghijduvānī and Khoja Aḥmad Yasavī, respectively, two of the successors of Shaykh Yūsuf Hamadānī. The latter's genealogy, curiously, is traced back to the Imām Abū Ḥanīfah and thence to Adam through Gayomart and the other figures of Iranian tradition.

Finally, after this exposition of his father's *silsilah* links, the author concludes that although the figures mentioned were the *pīrs* of the Sayyid's training and education, his father was in reality an Uvaysī, guided by the spirits of countless great saints; he thus has recourse to the notion of the Uvaysī Sufis, a concept known from the early centuries of Islam but evidently developed most extensively in Central Asian Naqshbandī circles, to in effect "universalize" his father's spiritual training beyond even the wide scope of *silsilahs* traced in the work.

The second *maqām* (IO ff. 30b-47a, Raza ff. 38b-59a) covers the life of Sayyid Jamāl ad-Dīn, outlining the major travels of his life and noting the major figures with whom he associated. The account begins with the death of Sayyid Pādshāh Khoja and Khoja Bābā's training of Sayyid Jamāl ad-Dīn, complete with such standard hagiographical features as dreams of the deceased Sayyid Pādshāh Khoja, comparisons with major events from the lives of other Sufis, and stories of Khoja Bābā's life among the beasts of the desert. We learn that Sayyid Jamāl ad-Dīn was raised for twelve years under the guidance of Khoja Bābā, and maintained contact also with the latter's brother Sayyid Muḥammad before beginning the travels that took him eventually to India.

Stories are related of his visits to Marv and his meetings with the *majdhūb* Sufi Bābā Chūpān, and his encounters in Balkh with Khoja ʿAbd al-Hādī, a successor of Khoja Muḥammad Pārsā, and with the eminent jurist Mawlānā Saʿīd Turkistānī. At some point he traveled to Bukhara, where he became acquainted with Khoja-yi Kalān Dahbīdī as well as with "Khoja-yi Jūybārī," in whose home he met the "*pādshāh* of the age," ʿAbdullāh Khan; the absence of chronological indications makes it unclear whether *the* "Khoja Jūybārī," i.e. Khoja Islām (d. 971/1563), or his son Khoja Saʿd (d. 997/1589), is to be understood here. Some idea of chronology, as well as of how much of Sayyid Jamāl ad-Dīn's life in Central Asia is not covered by the present work, is provided in the account of the *shaykh*'s journey to Balkh after leaving Bukhara with the intention of performing the *ḥajj*; the author mentions Pīr Muḥammad Khan (d. 974/1567), son of Jānī-Beg Sulṭān, as the ruler of Balkh, and notes his father's association with Jān Khoja (d. 995/1587), a descendant of Khoja Muḥammad Pārsā.

The remainder of the second *maqām* deals with Sayyid Jamāl ad-Dīn's journey to and residence in India. Following the dual blows to the usual *ḥajj*-routes of Central Asian pilgrims entailed by the establishment of the Ṣafavid state in Iran and by the Russian conquest of Astrakhan a half-century later, India provided the chief avenue for pilgrims from Central Asia on their way to Mecca, and Sayyid Jamāl ad-Dīn's intended route clearly reflected this pattern. After departing from Balkh, Sayyid Jamāl ad-Dīn traveled through Sind, where he remained for some time, and eventually decided to begin the *ḥajj* by ship from Sind via Hormuz and Basra; his party set off at the time of the monsoons, however, and the ship was driven aground and wrecked in a storm. Sayyid Jamāl ad-Dīn and, we are told, a four-month-old child named Badr Muḥammad Khoja reached shore safely and began a journey through deserts and wastes that led them finally to Agra. There they were well-received and cared for by an *amīr* in the service of Akbar, but Sayyid Jamāl ad-Dīn soon sought to travel to Gujarat, presumably to continue on his pilgrimage; the author tells of his move to Gujarat, first to Baroda and finally to Sūrat, where he remained for the rest of his life, except for an unspecified time spent in Burhānpūr at the behest of Akbar's son, prince Dānīyāl, as is learned in the third *maqām*; his residence in Burhānpūr most probably occurred in or after 1601, when Dānīyāl was appointed viceroy of the region (including Gujarat).

The third *maqām*, comprising the bulk of the work (IO ff. 47a-102a, Raza ff. 59a-121a), presents a series of anecdotes, with no apparent chronological or organizational principle and no narrative link, relating the wondrous deeds and miracles of Sayyid Jamāl ad-Dīn. Names of rulers and Sufis, as well as of the places which served as the settings for most stories, are given only incidentally; they allow, nevertheless, interesting glimpses of the activity, travels, and connections of the Sayyid.

From these anecdotal accounts we get some idea of the extensive links between Central Asia and India in terms of the "exchange" of Sufi talent; we find a steady stream of *shaykh*s with Central Asian *nisbah*s and with Yasavī, Naqshbandī, and other *silsilah* links, traveling in Gujarat and other Moghul domains; we find frequent reference to the still-powerful descendants of the pivotal 12th-century Khurasānī Sufi Shaykh Aḥmad-i Jām; we find further anecdotes centered upon the Jūybārī and Dahbīdī Khojas and other Central Asian Naqshbandī *shaykh*s; we learn of the Sayyid's links with various princes of Khorezm (e.g. Shāh Qulī Sulṭān, ʿAlī Sulṭān), with *amīr*s of Shāh Tahmāsp, and with Akbar's sons (especially Dānīyāl and Sulṭān Timūr) and *amīr*s (including a certain Shīr Khoja Sayyid Atāʾī).

Other anecdotes help somewhat with chronology, making it likely, for instance, that Sayyid Jamāl ad-Dīn's stay in Bukhara came during ʿAbdullāh Khan's reign but still during the lifetime of the latter's father Iskandar Khan (d. 1583); this, coupled with the earlier mention of Pīr Muḥammad Khan as ruler of Balkh, confirms that Sayyid Jamāl ad-Dīn's departure from Central Asia may have occurred as early as the mid-1560s, and if so we may speculate that his move to Gujarat from Agra may have been connected with the Moghul conquest of Gujarat in 1573. The growing European presence on the Indian coast is reflected in another extended anecdote, relating a further attempt at performing the *ḥajj* in which Sayyid Jamāl ad-Dīn (together with his pupil and eventual biographer Akhūnd Mawlānā Darvīsh Tāshkandī) was shipwrecked in a storm soon after departing from Sūrat. The pilgrims' ship was driven ashore in the *vilāyat-i farang*, undoubtedly the Portuguese enclaves of Gujarat, and the ship and all its cargo were seized by the *farangī*s. The pilgrims themselves were treated well and led to the port of Daman, from which they were eventually returned to Mīrzā Dūst Muḥammad, the governor of Sūrat.

Likewise in the context of an anecdote on a particular miracle of the Sayyid, we learn that he held lands in India as *soyurghal*; unfortunately no further details are given which might clarify the structure and extent of the Sayyid's landholdings. The third *maqām* of the work is thus a rich, but often frustrating, source which deserves careful analysis in conjunction with contemporary Central Asian and Indian historical, administrative, and hagiographical works.

The fourth *maqām* (IO ff. 102a-116a, Raza ff. 121a-135b) is devoted to a brief presentation of the "holy utterances" (*kalimāt-i qudsīyah*) of Sayyid Jamāl ad-Dīn, including a number of his poems and prayers. Most of the discourses recounted in this section deal with elements of Yasavī tradition, most notably the issue of the vocal *dhikr* and its permissibility.

Finally, the *khātimah* (IO ff. 116a-126b [abrupt ending], Raza ff. 135b-147b) relates the circumstances of Sayyid Jamāl ad-Dīn's death. After a final journey, in 1015/1606-07, to Aḥmadābād and then Burhānpūr, on the command of the new *sulṭān* Jahāngīr, Sayyid Jamāl ad-Dīn returned to Sūrat and died there on the eve of Friday, 5 Ṣafar 1016 (i.e. Thursday evening, 31 May 1607). He was buried at his *khānqāh* in Sūrat, and following several anecdotes on wondrous events associated with his grave, and a series of *ta'rīkh*s and *qaṣīdah*s in praise of the Sayyid, the author again identifies himself and the date of his completion of the work (1036/1626).

Despite its richness, the *Manāqib al-akhyār* is a relatively isolated example of Yasavī hagiography; it is not cited in later works, and with few exceptions the only earlier hagiographical works its author cites are of Naqshbandī provenance. It is, I would suggest, another clear example of the growing Naqshbandī domination of Central Asian Sufism, as that *ṭarīqah*, its *silsilah*, and its intellectual and social traditions came to pervade the existing Sufi brotherhoods and either compete with them or absorb them. In the evidence the *Manāqib al-akhyār* provides on the currency of Naqshbandī formulations of doctrinal principles; in its author's allusion to competition from Naqshbandī groups for influence at court; in his appeal to the Uvaysī idea to enhance his father's spiritual pedigree; and in the work's attestation of the appeal of Khoja Aḥrār to the Sayyid Atā'ī "Khoja Baba" and his brother, we find reflections of the competitive advantage increasingly enjoyed by Naqshbandī circles in Central Asia. The latter point - Khoja Aḥrār's appeal to adepts who belonged to a hereditarily defined Sufi lineage - is of particular interest, illuminating for us the shift away from family-based Sufi organizations of an earlier era, such as were characteristic of the initial Yasavī *silsilah*-lines, and toward actual Sufi *ṭarīqah*s of the classic type, as exemplified by the Naqshbandīyah.

I have elsewhere[13] outlined the evidence of competition with and imitation of the Naqshbandī order in the case of the Kubravīyah, on the basis of two Central Asian Kubravī hagiographies (the *Miftāḥ aṭ-ṭālibīn* and the *Jāddat al-ʿāshiqīn*) which predate the *Manāqib al-akhyār* by 50-75 years; the latter work confirms that the doctrinal preeminence of the Naqshbandīyah was clearly felt in Yasavī circles as well as in the Central Asian Kubravīyah. In this regard it is worth noting that despite the adoption of Naqshbandī principles and doctrinal emphases, what is jealously guarded in works of Yasavī provenance, both doctrinal and hagiographical, is the validity of the essential practical method associated with the Yasavīyah, the vocal *dhikr*.

We cannot further explore here the wealth of material preserved in this virtually unknown source; our aim has been merely to call attention to the *Manāqib al-akhyār* as a rich source of information on Central Asian history and Central Asian contacts with Moghul India

[13] "The Eclipse of the Kubravīyah in Central Asia," *Iranian Studies*, 21/1-2 (1988), pp. 45-83.

during the 16th and early 17th centuries. The work deserves special attention for its distinctive perspective on social history, a perspective which hagiographies often afford but which is only rarely found in court histories and chronicles. It is as a rare source on an otherwise unknown branch of the Yasavīyah, however, that the work is most valuable, for in addition to illustrating the broader religious environment in 16th-century Central Asia, with the growing penetration of Naqshbandī ideals and influence into non-Naqshbandī orders, it also reveals the wide range and appeal of the Yasavī legacy; with the enormous impact of that legacy in Central Asia, and its "rediscovery" in the post-Soviet era, the Yasavī heritage deserves careful analysis on the basis of a substantial number of little-known and still-untapped sources such as the one outlined here.

ON THE CREATIVE METHOD

OF MEDIEVAL UZBEK LITERATURE

A. Khaiitmetov

During the middle ages the peoples of Central Asia, including the Uzbek people, achieved considerable successes in the field of culture, particularly in the field of artistic creation. World-class status was attained by the Tajik, Uzbek, and Turkmen literatures, in the works of ʿAbd ar-Raḥmān Jāmī (15th century), ʿAlī-shīr Navāʾī (15th century), and Makhtumquli (18th century), respectively.

A characteristic feature of these literatures was their reflection of critical problems. Their expression of many social problems is testimony to the communicative service provided by literature to the people.

The development of these literary traditions was shaped by numerous factors, including old and new native traditions as well as traditions of other literatures which greatly influenced their development. This attests to the idea that the development of the literature of Central Asian peoples has had its internal regularities and development, and that its achievements have never been coincidental or unexpected.

The Uzbek literature of the medieval period is rich and various with respect to genre. It has its own peculiarities and its own artistic principles.

In the creative work of its representatives there are common and individual elements. For example, the poet Atāʾī differs in his poetic style from Sakkākī, and Sakkākī is not similar to Luṭfī. But they are united by the positive attitude to the traditional themes and images, by their echoing of certain ideas and even details in their creative work, by their borrowing in poetic depiction, and by their imitating the poems of their favorite poets and teachers. By their creative work they all tried, according to their abilities, to answer the demands of the time as well as those of literature and poetry, as was manifested in the community of their aspirations. ʿAlī-shīr Navāʾī in many respects surpassed his predecessors and contemporaries; but despite this, his creative works, and especially his *ghazal*s, have much in common with lyric poetry of the predecessors from the standpoint of idea, theme, and image. The prevalence of *ghazal*s on the theme of love, constituting dozens of poetical *dīvān*s of Uzbek poets, speaks of the common artistic principles of lyric poetry of the medieval period, characteristic of their creative method.

The creative method of the literatures of the peoples in the East has been discussed and written about in a number of interesting works by such great Soviet scholars and writers as A. Fadeev, Samed Vurgun, Sadriddin Aini, Mirza Ibragimov, N. I. Konrad, G. I. Lomidze, I. S. Braginskii, V. Iu. Zakhidov, I. Z. Nurulin, I. A. Sultanov, A. Gadzhiev, N. Mallaev, G. Karimov, Ya. Garaev and others. But the issue has not reached its full, comprehensive scholarly resolution. Ongoing research in this direction is being carried out by the author of these lines.[1]

In the epoch under consideration, poetry was the prevalent form in Uzbek literature, especially secular, lyric poetry. The main focus of the lyric was, as is well-known, love, the outer beauty of the beloved, the inexhaustible feeling of the lover (*ʿāshiq*), the lover's devotion, his suffering in parting with the beloved, his deep emotion and profound thoughts, etc. The Uzbek poets, including Alisher Navoi, used such bright "colors" - metaphors, hyperbole, etc. - in their artistic verse rendering of all these elements and others, that very often the images of main characters and the description of their condition became exaggerated and too elevated. Let me give one example. Luṭfī, writing about the tears in the eyes of his character, compares his tearful eyes with the full-flowing river Jayḥūn (that is, the Amu Darya):

lab ba-lab vaṣlin tiläb, tāpmān kanārïn nečakim,
közlerim ol yašïnï ḥasratda jayḥūn äylädi[2]

I swim [through the river of separation] seeking
reunion [with my beloved], but do not find the
shore,
In pain my blood-filled tears form a [new] Jayḥūn.[3]

[1] I have published the following monographs on this problem: *Nävaiyning ijadiy metodi mäsäläläri* (Tashkent, 1963); *Shärq ädäbiyatining ijadiy metodi tärikhidän* (Tashkent, 1970).

[2] Lutfiy, *Devan. Gul vä Nävruz* (Tashkent, 1966), p. 288.

[3] (English translations from the verses cited reflect the author's interpretation as indicated in the Russian translations provided in the text [DD]).

The comparison here is, without doubt, hyperbolic, but it is characteristic of medieval lyric poetry.

Therefore, in my opinion, those investigators who consider the method of these poets non-realistic, or more precisely, romantic, are correct. In the prevailing idealistic outlook the progressive romantic artistic method dominated among leading poets and facilitated the development of the literature, and the exaltment of life-affirming ideas and of humanism.

The poet, and his lyric hero in his *ghazal*s, in many cases expresses his attitude toward his own concrete, historical time, toward events, and toward actual people through the theme of love and by hints and allusions, etc. Uzbek poets of that period were guided by humanist ideals in their creative work. They glorified earthly love, the beauty of life, and love of reality and of man, as opposed to religious views and dogmas. The most characteristic and general feature in their composition of *ghazal*s was that, having isolated themselves in the world of the love lyric, the world of *ghazal*s, they virtually denied the "dignity" of real socio-political contemporary life, and did not see in it anything positive or beautiful that deserved to be described or praised by them; love of man, his outer and inner beauty, and the deep emotions of the lover all seemed to these poets to be the highest consideration. They looked at the world and at life in many respects unilaterally, through the eyes of their lyric heroes, the lovers.

Occasionally we come across *ghazal*s that were written under the influence of real life situations, as if responding to them, with *ghazal*s describing real images of the people contemporary to the poet. Such is the case in one of Navāʾī's *ghazal*s, beginning with the following two lines:

tāmīda ermäs kabūtar khayli bu jurʿat bilä,
kim parīlär keldi ʿāshiqlïqqa ol ṣūrat bilä.[4]

The doves who seek to sit atop his house are not
doves,

[4] Älisher Nävaiy, *Khäzayinul-mäani*, vol. 3, *Badae'ul-väsät* (Tashkent, 1960), p. 538.

But *parī*-like lovers who have taken the form of
doves.

Here Navāʾī describes the habit of Sulṭān Ḥusayn Bayqarā, who according to the testimony of Bābur enjoyed himself with dove-playing and goat-tearing. However, the poet depicts him not in the direct realistic manner, but in the image of traditional beloved, who enjoys herself among *parī*-like doves.

Another *ghazal* by Navoi begins with the two lines:

ne lūlīvašdur ol qātil ke qan tökmäkkädur yaksar
qïya baqmaqlarï pāki itik mujgānlarï naštar.

That gypsy-like killer who slays his own lovers,
Resembles a knife with his piercing glance, a lance
with his eyelashes.

This, according to Bābur, refers to various acrobatic games and tricks of a certain Gypsy lad; Navāʾī enjoyed his skillful games and went to watch him from time to time.[5] In such poems are reflected more or less real people and their deeds and actions, but not their direct and realistic representation.

To this type of poem one can attribute the following *ghazal* by Navāʾī, where in traditional style is described the process of embroidering a man's belt kerchief; as the lover wholeheartedly admires the skillful work of his sweetheart, the poet gives us a picture of everyday life in romantic colors against the background of the traditional theme of love:

yaglïgïn, ey-kim, tikärsen, ignä mujgānïmnï qïl.
naqš etärda tārï anïng rišta-i jānïmnï qïl.
istäsäng tārïn qïzïl yākhūd qara qïlmaqqa rang,
köz qarasïn hal qïlïb, közdin aqar qanïmnï qïl.

[5] Babir, *Mukhtäsär* (Tashkent, 1971), p. 127.

gar desäng har yan qïzïl gullär qïlay nuṣḥat anga,
köksüm ačïp, tāza qanlïġ daġï hijrānïmnï qïl.
ġunčalar gul yanïda tikmäk taḥayyul äyläsäng,
anga nuṣḥat köngül atlïġ zārï ḥayrānïmnï qïl . . .[6]

Make a hair of my eylash your needle for
embroidery,
And take the thread of my soul as the design for
your work.
If you want to color the thread black or red,
Trace the pupil of my eye and use the blood it
sheds.
And if you wish to embroider red roses along each
edge,
Open my bosom and make them of my fresh blood.
If you want to sew red rosebuds around them,
Make them from the heart of this one slain by you.

The progressiveness and vitality evident in the poetry of the poets of that period, as well as their creative method and their activity lay in the fact that they were leading figures concerned about their people, their country, and its future. That is why their creative work represented many of life's contradictions in a peculiar, indirect way. As a whole, they put forward an active humanistic ideal, personified in the lyric character of their poems. In doing so, they hoped by the strength of their convictions to change and improve the society and to influence the conscience of the exploiters. In spite of the illusory nature of their positive program, protest against their contemporary social establishment played an outstanding role in the spiritual development of the people. The lyric hero of Navā'ī is characteristic in this respect. Lamenting the unbearable conditions of his epoch, in one of his *ghazals* he comes to the conclusion that God should recreate the world according to desires of the people:

[6] Älisher Nävaiy, *Khäzayinul-mäani*, vol. 4, *Fävaidul-kibär* (Tashkent, 1960), p. 378.

gar bu-dur ʿālam, kišigä mumkin ermäs anda kām
ḥaqq magar-kim kām učun baštīn yaratqay ʿālam-e.[7]
Insofar as the world was created without the
possibility for man to achieve his desires,
God should create the world anew, according to
peoples' wishes.

These thoughts about the socio-political system of his epoch lead the lyric hero of Navoi to the denial of the system, elevating him far above his time. The same can be said about the lyric characters of other Uzbek poets. The creative method called by us conventional, romantic, and progressive allowed sufficient possibility to remain in those medieval conditions to think relatively freely in poetry, to transcend the needs of everyday life, to look boldly into the future, and to dream of changing the world, overthrowing oppression, and ensuring a free life for the people.

The romantic character in medieval Uzbek literature, especially in poetry, is traceable still more clearly on the example of the romantic, heroic, and adventure poetry of the period.

Authors set as the basis of their poems not real events of their time, but events of a fairy-tale character and legends and traditions from historical chronicles. In their poetic practice they creatively mastered many conceptual artistic principles and folkloric images. Very often they resorted to the folk legends about Yūsuf and Zuleikhā, Gul and Navrūz, Farhād and Shīrīn, Laylī and Majnūn and others. As an example, Durbek, as he composed his poem about Yūsuf and Zuleikhā, was in Balkh, which was under siege by the enemy. He witnessed all the suffering of the city's defenders and admired their courage; and, as he composed the poem on a topic borrowed from religious books, Durbek was able to introduce into it a secular and contemporary spirit by which he sought to morally support the exhausted citizens; for the main characters of the poem, as well as the citizens, experienced suffering and torment but, overcoming them, reached prosperity and happiness. Thus did the poet create his work in allegorical form.

[7] Älisher Nävaiy, *Khäzayinul-mäani*, vol. 2, *Nävadirush-shäbab* (Tashkent, 1959), p. 580.

ʿAlī-shīr Navāʾī continued and developed the romantic tendency in poetic composition in his *Khamsa.* This is clearly seen in his poem "Farhād and Shīrīn," which the poet based on folkloric rather than literary material. Farhād is a man of rare qualities (*nādir yigit āfāq ičindä*); in the poem he is represented not only as passionate lover, but as warrior, a skillful stonecutter, and a scholar - a combination hardly compatible in a single man in reality. During his campaign in Greece he defeats the monster Ahriman, a great Dragon, and stone robots; in Armenia he single-handedly cuts the canal through the mountains, fulfilling the wish of his beloved, and alone he bars the way to the troops of the Shah Khusraw of Iran. There are many conventional features in the artistic-poetic representation of Farhād and other characters in the poem and of natural scenes, etc. And such a poem can hardly be called realistic as asserted by some of our scholars.

The same can be said about the poem "Laylī and Majnūn." In the image of love-sick Majnūn (that is, "mad with love"), Navāʾī - as did Niẓāmī, Dihlavī, Jāmī, and Fużūlī - represents a man of pure, exalted soul with all strong emotion and deep meditation inherent within him. Majnūn, rejected by Laylī's parents, goes into the steppe, isolates himself, and shares his sorrows with animals. In describing the state of the unhappy lover the poet uncovers beautiful scenes before the reader, uses wonderfully detailed imagery, and plays with inimitable nuances of romantic representation. Once, near the camp where Laylī was dwelling, Majnūn saw the smoke of the hearth, and said:

čïqsa edi ol qabīladïn dūd,
äylär edi közni sūrma andūd.[8]

He saw the black smoke in his grief,
And it served as collyrium for his eyes.

This is only one scene from the poem. Impetuous romanticism in this work is evident not only in the heroes' rejection of the social

[8] Älisher Nävai, *Khämsä* (Tashkent, 1960), p. 432.

environment, in descriptions of their unconventional deeds, but also in the poetics and style of the author's portrayals.

The fourth poem of Navāʾī's *Khamsa* is of the romantic-adventure type. Many stories in it remind us of folk-tales. In the poem about Iskandar, Navāʾī goes even further in this direction. The poet attributes a positive sense to Iskandar's conquests. In the author's conception, Iskandar conquers the whole world not for the sake of personal enrichment and fame, but in order to establish universal justice. All the campaigns of Iskandar are described in the elevated poetic style typically characteristic of heroic poems, Except for certain elements, Iskandar's image is as a whole romantic, sometimes fantastic. The poet attributes to him the distinctive features of an educated and just ruler and an invincible military leader. This image only outwardly recalls the historical personality of Alexander the Great, the cruel conqueror of Central Asia and other countries; in this image are personified high ideals about the just and enlightened ruler. In this poem the romantic style of Navāʾī attained the highest tones and colors.

Of the same character is the poem "Gul and Navrūz" by Luṭfī, as well as "The Legend of Sayf al-Mulūk" by Majlisī. In the poem of Nishāṭī (18th century) called "*Ḥusn-u-dil*" after the names of its main characters - "Beauty" and "Heart" - there appear also such characters as Passion (*ʿishq*), Reason (*ʿaql*), Thought (*khayāl*), Tenderness (*nāz*), Figure (*qāmat*), Fear (*vahm*), and others. This shows that conventionality and allegory have a significant place in the tradition of artistic representation in Uzbek poetry.

It should be added that one more distinctive feature in the style of progressive romantic poetry is the skillful combination of the predominant elevated style with a realistic one. For example, when Navāʾī is describing his native Khurāsān, he does so not abstractly, but in a real and concrete fashion.

Some scholars consider that in approaching the method of medieval Uzbek literature it is proper to refer to a "romantic tendency." However, in this writer's opinion, this is not quite correct, since "tendency" can denote the artistic method of undeveloped literatures, literary traditions just being formed.

A final question is appropriate: did realism exist as a method in medieval Uzbek literature? In this writer's view, realism was not the leading artistic method in medieval Uzbek literature; but a realistic tendency may be observed in this literature. A number of genres tended to realism. Works of a didactic character, poems of satirical and autobiographical character, works of historical content, such as the *Bābur-nāmah* by Bābur, Abū'l-Ghāzī's *Shajarah-i Turk*, or Muḥammad Ṣāliḥ's *Shaybānī-nāmah*, were chiefly oriented toward the representation of real life and existing socio-political and cultural events, as well as toward the description of historical, concrete personalities. Concerning such works it may not be inappropriate to use the term "realistic tendency," because realism here is not yet completely creative, but is rather descriptive. (In these works are depicted the facts that exist or have existed, but the characters and events are not recreated).

In medieval Uzbek literature, in the persons of Navā'ī, Luṭfī, Bābur, Mu'nis, and others, there are some strong, instructive aspects, as well as weak elements. The emotional, romantically elevated, brightly expressive, artistically superior side of their creative work - this is the valuable component worth examining in our time. Scholarly study and the generalization of experience for both the realistic and romantic elements in our classics is an essential undertaking for the development of contemporary literature. It is suggested that this problem ought to be investigated with a more thorough and multi-sided approach.

THE LEXICO-SEMANTIC FIELD OF WRITTEN LANGUAGE IN OLD TURKIC, OLD UZBEK, AND MODERN UZBEK

Iristai K. Kuchkartaev

There were two instruments for writing in use among the Turks of the Old Turkic period: *pir* (a brush made of hair) and *qalam* (reed pen). The word *pir* was borrowed from the Chinese Language in the form *pit/bit*; the word *qalam* was adopted together with the Sogdian, Uyghur, Syrian, Manichean and Brahmi scripts.[1]

According to A. von Gabain, in Manichean and Nestorian works the notion of "book" was expressed by the word *petka*. Its derivative *petkačï*, meaning "scribe," was used in the form *bitkači*; but this word was not widely used in the Old Turkic language.

From the substantive *pit/bit*, borrowed from Chinese, the Turks formed the verb *biti-/piti-* (to cut out an inscription, to write): *taš bitidim* ("I have inscribed an inscription on a stone"), *tört kün olurup bitidim* (I have been cutting out an inscription for four days"). The verb *biti-* may be found not only in the monuments of the Turkic runic script but in those of Uyghur and other scripts as well.

The widespread use of the verb *biti-* in Old Turkic is confirmed by the presence of a number of its derivatives and compounds: *bitig* ("book," "inscription," "document"), *bitigči* ("scribe"), *bitigäči* ("scribe"), *bitiglig* ("someone with good handwriting"), *bitiglig* ("written," "relating to written language"), *bitiglig* ("literate"), *bitigü* ("ink"), *bitigsiz* ("unwritten"), *bitimäk* ("writing"), *bititdäči* ("someone commissioning someone to correspond"), *bitigäči oğlan* ("pupil"), *bitig ček-* ("to dot letters above or below"), *bitig taš* ("a stone with an inscription, tombstone"), *baš bitig* ("chief document"), *kuyn bitig* ("scroll"), *nirvan bitig* (title of a Mahāyāna *sūtra*). From these examples it is clear that the aforementioned word *petkäčï* was changed into *bitkäči* on analogy with *bitigäči*, *bitigči* and similar derivatives of the verb *biti-*. The presence of a number of synonyms with the meaning "scribe" indicates that this profession was quite common in the Old Turkic period profession at that times; this is sug-

[1] A. von Gabain, "Kul'tura pis'ma v pechataniia u drevnikh tiurok," in *Zarubezhnaia tiurkologiia*, vyp. 1 (Moscow, 1986), pp. 161-162.

gested also by the word *ïlïmġa* ("a scribe in the khan's chancery"), attested in Old Turkic sources.

The verb *biti-*, conforming as it does to the phonetic and morphological structure of Turkic verbs, was quite readily adopted by Turkic languages and became the dominant lexical unit for denoting objects and phenomena connected with the spheres of the scribes's activity an written language. It is altogether curious that in subsequent periods this verb is used with both the open stem (*biti-*) and with the closed stem (*bit-*), thus assimilating with three phoneme structure of the Turkic root.

To the group of words in Old Turkic connected with writing and written language must be added one more verb, namely *yaz-* ("to write"), attested in the Turfan texts. This verb, however, did not enjoy widespread use in the Old Turkic language, unlike the Verb *biti-*; the local, limited use of *yaz-* in the Old Turkic period was noted by Maḥmūd Kāshgharī, who cited the example *ol bitig yazdï* ("he wrote a book") and observed that this word belonged to the Oghuz language.[2]

It may be appropriate to consider separately the group of words denoting the various genres of Old Turkic texts. Here above all must be noted the word *nom* ("book," "religious teaching," "writing"), borrowed from Sogdian, which was connected with a religion whose spread in the Turkic environment in this period is well attested in historical sources. This word was quite widespread in Old Turkic, as attested by its numerous derivatives and compounds: *nomla-* ("to preach," "to teach the law"), *nomluġ* ("referring to the law," "religion," "adhering to some doctrine"), *nomčï* ("preacher," "religious preceptor"), *nom bitig* ("writing," "book," "sutra"), *nom eligi* ("master-book"), *nom qutï* ("the greatness of the writing/religious law/faith"), *nom sazïn* ("religious precept"), *nom törü* ("law," "rule"). There were a number of other words connected with religious teachings, whose use was for some reason limited, e.g. *šasanï* ("dogma," "precept"); this word was borrowed from Sanskrit.

There was a small group of words denoting official documents: *basïġ* ("treaty," "appeal"), *tutsuġ* ("will," "testament"), *vaṣïyyat* ("will," "testament," "instruction").

[2] Mähmud Kashgäriy, *Devanu luġat it-turk*, I (Tashkent, 1960), p. 66.

In addition may be cited words referring to secular literature and its varieties: *kavi* ("poem," "epos"), *qošuġ* ("verse," "poem"), *qoš-* (fig. "to compose verses or songs"), *tüzät-* ("to compose verses"). The majority of these words encountered in written monuments of the Qarakhanid period: *ol yïr qošdï* ("he has written verses"), *bu türkčä qošuġlar tüzättim sängä* ("I have written these Turkic verses for you").

Yet another group of words in the lexical stock of the Old Turkic monuments, with meanings associated with incantations and magic, may be considered as a special variety of the lexico-semantic field of writing and written language, insofar as incantations were written upon household articles, sticks, amulets, etc. The dominant word in this group is *arva-* ("to conjure," "to utter incantations"), which had numerous derivatives and formed part of many compounds: *arvaš* ("incantation"), *arvïš* ("magic spell," "magic formula"), *arvïš* ("charm"), *arvïščï* ("magician," "charmer"), *arvïšlïġ* ("magical"), *arvïšlar eligi* ("king of knowledge"), *yelni arvïš* ("sorcery"), *darnï arvïs* ("magic formula," "incantation"). This group also involves the following words: *yat* ("sorcery to produce rain or wind"), *yatčï* ("sorcerer," "magician"), *yatla-* ("to conjure"), *yoġur-* ("to cast a spell," "to make an incantation"), *qam* ("shaman," "healer," "soothsayer," "magician," "charmer").

During the period of the flowering of Turkic literature in Central Asia, the system of norms and values which regulated the functioning of the literary language took new directions. This was the period in which was formed the Old Uzbek literary language formed, "which in its sources goes back to the norms and traditions of the old literary languages of Central Asia of the Qarakhanid epoch (Kashghar, Balasaghun, 11th-12th centuries), and of the Golden Horde period (the lower Syr Darya and Khorezm, 13th-14th centuries), and was enriched by the stream of lexical and grammatical innovations borrowed from the popular colloquial languages of the Turkic peoples of Central Asia."[3]

As the products of a rapidly developing literary language were embodied in words and discourse, the word, speech, and language

[3] A. N. Kononov, *Istoriia izucheniia tiurkskikh iazykov v Rossii; Dooktiabr'skii period* (Leningrad, 1982), pp. 282-283.

occupied a special place; this in turn led to the conscious veneration of the word, and especially the artistic, literary word, which we find in the sayings of the literary figures of that period about the role of words and language. The clearest representative of this is ʿAlī-shīr Navāʾī, the founder of the Old Uzbek literary language, who composed a special work (the *Muḥākamat al-lughatayn*) on the artistic and esthetic possiblities of Turkic words. It was he who was successful in propelling and orienting the literary process.[4] He "not only perfected the poetic genres and the corresponding poetic variant of the literary language; productively reworking the prose genres in the Central Asian Turkic literary language, he began the delimitation of the prose and poetic variants of the literary language."[5] Turkic-language literature in the Timurid states functioned as an entire system of diverse forms, variants, and genres of literary and esthetic expression.

Consequently special attention was devoted in the literary language to terms denoting the forms and genres of artistic literature, among which the terms *naẓm* and *nasr*, denoting the poetic and prose varieties of the single literary language, held a special place. Because poetic genres predominated in classical Uzbek literature, the word *naẓm* was used more extensively than the word *nasr*: *naẓm mulki* ("the world of poetry"), *naẓm ilmi* ("theory of versification"), *naẓm silkigä tart-* ("to render in poetic form"), *naẓm äylä-* ("to make verses"). The greater portion of literary terms was also connected with poetry: *šiʿr* ("poem"), *ghazal* ("lyric"), *rubāʿī* ("quatrain"), *mukhammas* ("five-lined verse"). But the group of terms connected with the prosaic variety of the language was not inconsiderable either, e.g. *risāla* ("treatise"), *qiṣṣa* ("story"). Words denoting different kinds of collected literary works became common elements of the language: *dīvān* ("collection of verse"), *tadhkira* ("anthology"), *bayāż* ("anthology," "collection"). The same may be said about the words connected with the various forms of official documents and the sphere

[4] S. E. Malov, "Mir Alisher Navoi v istorii tiurkskikh literatur i iazykov Srednei i Perednei Azii," *Izvestiia Akademii nauk, Otdelenie literatury i iazyka*, 1947, t. VI, vyp. 6, p. 480.

[5] G. F. Blagova, "O sootnosheniiakh prozaicheskogo i poèticheskogo variantov sredneaziatsko-tiurkskogo pis'menno-literaturnogo iazyka XV-nachala XVI v.," in *K semidesiatiletiiu akad. A. N. Kononova* (Leningrad, 1976), p. 30.

of clerical work: *maktūb* ("letter"), *khaṭṭ* ("letter"), *munshī* ("scribe," "secretary"), *kātib* ("secretary").

There was a special group of words as well for expressing the notion of "eloquence" and its various nuances: *faṣīḥ* ("eloquent, expressive language"), *faṣāḥat* ("eloquence"), *nuqṭa* ("witty remark"), *nāṭiq* ("orator"), *sukhanvar* ("orator," "eloquent speaker"), *sukhandān* ("orator").

Within the new system of norms and values encouraged by new spiritual inquiry in general and by the tendency toward artistic and esthetic assimilation of the world in particular, the meanings of many words gained new complexity through nuances and complementary shadings; such phenomena as secondary denomination and metaphor became very common and were deliberately used as stylistic devices. In this respect the semantic and functional development of words connected with magic and incantations is of particular interest. As noted earlier, in Old Turkic these words were employed only in their primary meaning and their use did not extend outside the world of the sorcerors, shamans, and magicians. In Old Uzbek they began to develop figurative meanings and came to be used with respect to real phenomena indicating their acquisition of secondary meanings. The word *žādū* (*jādū*), borrowed from Persian, meant "sorcerer" or "fortune-teller" in Old Turkic,[6] but in Old Uzbek we find numerous examples of its use in characterizing other types of people: *žādū-yi hind* ("Indian magician," i.e. Khusraw Dihlavī), *nargis-i žādū* ("eyes full of mischief"), *žādūluq* ("attractiveness"). Other words of this semantic group were used similarly: *siḥr* ("charm," "slyness"), *siḥr payvandliǧ* (magic; skillful work), *siḥr pardāz* ("magician," "skillful man"), *siḥr körgüzmäk* ("to charm," "to be sly"), *arbaǧ* ("incantation," "charm," "fascination," "lie," "deceit"), etc.

A characteristic feature of the lexical stock of Old Uzbek is that the composition of verses and the creation of literary works were denoted by a whole series of lexical units; in other words, there was no special word with the generic meaning "to write," "to create literary works," which might have united around itself all words or compounds connected with this meaning. It is quite curious, indeed, that words such as *ayt-* and *de-*, usually denoting spoken language and

[6] L. N. Gumilev, *Drevnie tiurki* (Moscow, 1967), pp. 85-86.

ordinary expression, were used in the Old Uzbek literary language to refer to verse composition and artistic literary production as well: *šiʿr ayt-* ("to write poetry"), *ghazal ayt-* ("to write a gazel"), *badīʿa ayt-* ("to write fiction"), *qaṣīda ayt-* ("to write an ode"), *marthīya ayt-* ("to write an elegy"), *turkāna ayt-* ("to write in Turkic"), *šiʿr de-* ("to write poetry"), *abyāt de-* ("to write verses"). A number of word combinations with the words *qalam* ("pen") and *naẓm* ("poetry") also belonged to this group: *qalam sal-* ("to write"), *qalam ur-* ("to write, make notes"), *naẓm qïl-* ("to write verses"), *naẓm-kaš* ("poet").

As for the verbs *bit[i]-* and *yaz-*, they are used in Navāʾī's works primarily to denote the process of composing, writing, and rewriting letters and official communications; for this reason they are combined with nouns such as *maktūb* ("letter," "message"), *khaṭṭ* ("letter") *nāma* ("letter," "book"), *ariža-dāšt* ("petition"), etc. (cf. his *Munshaʾāt*). When they are used with regard to artistic literature, they indicate not the process of creating such works, but to their copying, collection, or other technical handling: *öz khaṭṭlarï bilä bitilgän dīvān* ("the *dīvān* which he compiled in his own handwriting"), *on mingdin artuqraq mathnavīsi bar, bayāżġa yazmaġanï üčün šuhrat tutmadï* ("he has more than ten thousand *mathnavī*s, but because he did not compile them in a collection they did not become famous").

The lexico-semantic field of the written language in Modern Uzbek differs from those of Old Uzbek and Old Turkic. The dominant word here is the verb *yaz-* which has two meanings: 1) to express and record by writing: *khät yaz-* ("to write a letter"), *ärizä yaz-* ("to write an application"); 2) to create or compose literary works: *šiʿr yaz-* ("to write poetry"), *äsär yaz-* ("to write a book"). In the first case the meaning of the Modern Uzbek verb *yaz-* almost coincides with that of the Old Uzbek *yaz-*. In the second case its meaning is close to that of the Old Uzbek verbs *ayt-* and *de-* as they were used in Navāʾī's works. The use of the verb *yaz-* in the meaning "to create or compose works" has been considerably extended in Modern Uzbek due to the verb's use in compounds with names of new things: *dissertatsia yaz-* ("to write a dissertation"), *mäqalä yaz-* ("to write an article"), *referat yaz-* ("to write a synopsis"), *därslik yaz-* ("to write a textbook"), etc. From the above we may conclude that the verb *yaz-* has the most general meaning among the words of the lexico-semantic filed under consideration. Its derivatives denoting and characterizing varieties of the written language confirm this: *yazuv* ("inscription," "record" "written language"), *yazuv-čizuv* ("writing," "scribble;" "document"), *yazišmä* ("correspondence"), *yazmä* ("written," "manuscript" [adj.]), *yazuvli* ("inscription-bearing"), *qolyazmä* ("manuscript"). From the stem *yaz-* the verbal noun *yazuvči* was derived and is now the chief generic designation for the profession and occupation of the writer.

The Modern Uzbek language has a rich vocabulary and a well developed system of functional styles. The following words are used to denote different varieties and styles of Modern Uzbek: *yazmä nutq* ("written language"), *aġzäki nutq* ("spoken language"), *ilmiy uslub* ("scientific style"), *bädiiy uslub* ("artistic-literary style"), *mätbuat tili* ("journalistic language"), etc. The lexical stock of Modern Uzbek, and especially its terminology, has been enriched by borrowings from other languages, above all from Russian and through Russian; many words are changing their meanings, being adapted to new conditions of life and to new concepts and things. This reflects a natural process of the "intellectualization" of the literary language in the contemporary circumstances of the scientific-technical revolution.

The diversity and intellectual saturation of the contemporary Uzbek language are attested by a number of words denoting various ways of expressing scientific thought: *tävsiflä-* "(to describe," "to characterize"), *täsvirlä-* ("to describe, to outline, to depict), *kharakterlä-* ("to characterize"), *i͗zahlä-* ("to explain," "to interpret"), *šärhlä-* ("to interpret," "to comment"), *i͗sbat* ("proof," "confirmation"), *i͗sbatlä-* ("to prove"), *jäkun* ("total"), *jäkunlä-* ("to sum up"), *doklad* ("report"), *doklad qil-* ("to make a report"). It should be noted that these words could be used with respect to the spoken language too.

Yet another characteristic of the lexical stock of the contemporary Uzbek literary language is the common use of two or more words to designate certain concepts and phenomena; ordinarily one of these words is traditional for Uzbek, while the other is new, borrowed or newly created on the basis of the language's internal resources. As examples may be cited the following words associated with literary discourse: *näzm* and *poèsiya* ("poetry"), *näsr* and *proza* ("prose"), *uslub* and *stil'* ("style"), *dastan* and *poèma* ("poem"), *muällif* and *avtor* ("author"), *muhärrir* and *redaktor* ("editor"). The presence of two or more words for indicating one and the same concept permits their stylistically differentiated use; at the same time, it serves to allow for greater preciseness and concreteness for associated ideas.

The characteristics and functions of words and expressions etymologically connected with magic and incantations have in Modern Uzbek found still further reinterpretation. The word *avra-*, a metathesized form of the word which in Old Turkic was the dominant term in this group, has in the contemporary Uzbek literary language lost its original meaning "to charm," "to cast a spell;" rather, it is used in the sense of "to deceive," "to cheat," "to trick," clearly representing reconceptualizations of the word's basic meaning. It may be noted here that some contemporary dictionaries portray the meaning "to deceive" as the basic and primary meaning of the verb *avra-*, while its original sense is given as a secondary meaning, inverting the facts of the word's history.

The word *avra-* in its secondary meaning has a number of derivatives in Modern Uzbek: *avrab-savrab* ("behaving deceitfully"), *avraqči* ("deceiver"). A certain semantic connection may be traced between Modern Uzbek *ävraqči* and Old Uzbek *arbaġ*, attested in the works of Navāʾī with the meaning "lie," "deception."[7]

As noted, the words *žādū* and *siḥr* ("magic," "charm") and their derivatives were used in the works of Navāʾī both in their original and secondary meanings (in which they denoted attractiveness, artificiality, and cunning). This is directly paralleled in the contemporary Uzbek literary language: *žadu* ("magic," "charm;" "charming," "attractive"), *žadu kozlär* ("bewitching eyes"), *žadugär* ("magician," "sly," "cruel"), *sehr* ("magic," "charm;" fascination), *sehrgär* ("charmer," "magician;" "skillful"), *soz sehrgäri* ("master of words," "good orator"), *sehrlä-* ("to charm," "to attract"), *sehrli* ("charmed," "bewitched;" "fascinating," "charming," "wonderful").

The comparative analysis of the method of superimposition of the systems of meanings noted above connected with the lexico-semantic field of the written language in Old Turkic, Old Uzbek and Modern Uzbek reveals the following pattern: the system of designations

[7] A. K. Borovkov, ed. and tr., *Bada'i al-lugat; slovar' Tali Imani Geratskogo* (Moscow, 1961), pp. 57-58.

adopted at a particular stage of language development is not displaced or discarded by that of subsequent stages, but is rather continued and maintained either as an essential element or as a relic of previous periods. The peripheral elements of the system are subjected to the strongest changes, both quantitative and qualitative; the central "kernels" of the system are preserved with insignificant changes both in content and expression.

The Old Turkic system of terminology for written languge had its "kernel," the dominant verb *biti-* and, at the secondary level, the verb *yaz-*, as well as other words; the Old Uzbek system had as its key elements the verb *ayt-* in the meaning "compose," "create," and the verbs *biti-* and *yaz-* in the meaning "to create a text in writing;" and the Modern Uzbek system has its own semantic kernel, namely the dominant verb *yaz-* in two meanings: 1) to create a text in writing, and 2) "to create," "to compose."

Thus, at each stage of the development of language in general, and of a literary language in particular, conditioned by the spiritual and cultural development of society, there occurs not a rejection or discarding of the previous system, but a reconceptualization and redistribution of the semantic and functional stock existing within the linguistic material of the system; this provides additional convincing evidence for continuity in the development of language and for its receptivity to changes in the life of the bearers of the language.

THE SEMANTIC-SYNTACTIC MECHANISM OF THE UZBEK COMPARATIVE SENTENCE

Nizamiddin Mamadalievich Makhmudov

The model semantics of a sentence determines the semantic-syntactic mechanism of its components' interaction. For this reason, it is possible to assert that the semantic-syntactic mechanism of the comparative sentence differs from the corresponding mechanism of a sentence of a different semantic model. It is likewise indisputable today that the discovery of the semantic-syntactic mechanism in sentences with different semantics is one of the cardinal problems of linguistics.

It is well-known that in the semantic structure of comparative sentences the principle of comparison - one of the most widespread logical modes of cognition of the outside world, or logical categories - is reflected. Consequently, such sentences are standard in all languages of the world, but their structure and the regularities of their formation are, naturally, characterized by definite specific signs in each language. Despite this fact, there is still no research in Uzbek linguistics focused on the semantic and syntactic mechanisms of the simple comparative sentence. In the present paper we will attempt to discover such mechanisms of the Uzbek simple comparative sentences.

In studying the semantic-syntactic mechanisms of sentences, three aspects should be taken into consideration: 1) logical, 2) semantic, and 3) syntactic.

From the logical point of view, the structure of the statement in comparative sentences differs noticeably from that expressed in sentences of any other type. According to formal logic, where the conception of the binomial composition of the statement, going back to Aristotle's logic, is considered absolute, all statements without exception consist of two parts: subject and predicate. Is the composition of the statement the same in comparative sentences? M. I. Morozova stresses that "the structure of comparative statements differs from that of ordinary statements: completeness of thought in them depends not only on the two main parts of the statement, but also on a third, representing the second object of the comparison. If the structure of the binomial statement is "S - P," then the structure of the comparative statement is "S^1 - P - S^2."[1] As D. M. Potapova notes, "with the development of the formal logic, the classic Aristotelian understanding of the statement as the subject-predicate structure, in which the possession of some quality or sign by the object of thought is affirmed, was replaced by a more flexible understanding of the structure of the statement as a logical expression, allowing extensive relations according to the formula R (a,b), or a R b, or f(x,y)."[2] The question arises: how does such complexity in the structure of the statement appear in comparative sentences?

In formal logic, one of the principal means of drawing conclusions is the deduction, that is, the syllogism. Here a third statement is derived from two statements as a deduction. For example, from the statements "All planets are globe-shaped" and "The Earth is a planet," one may come to the conclusion that "The Earth is globe-shaped." This, naturally, is the full form of the syllogism, which consists of three parts: two bases and a conclusion.

As Aristotle pointed out, in creating a syllogism, if one part of it is well-known and obvious, it is not worth stating it, since the reader could add it himself; and in that case the syllogism obtains the form of an enthimema.[3]

Leaving the first foundation as a well-known fact of the above syllogism, one can obtain an enthimema in the form, "The Earth is a planet and therefore it is a globe-shaped." The logical basis and common sense are not altered when this enthimema is structured in the form, "The Earth is globe-shaped like all other planets." In this case only the form of expression of this information is subjected to change. It is seen very clearly that a comparative relation is expressed in the last form of the enthimema. Indeed, comparison lies at the foundation of every syllogism. Consequently, it is quite natural to present the forms of the enthimema in the shape of comparative sentences.

[1] M. I. Morozova, "Logika i sintaksis sravneniia," in *Grammatika i norma* (Moscow, 1977), p. 235.

[2] See M. P. Ionitsè and M. D. Potapova, *Problemy logiko-sintaksicheskoi organizatsii predlozheniia* (Kishinev, 1982), p. 22.

[3] Aristotel', "Ritorika," in *Antichnye ritoriki* (Moscow, 1978), pp. 22, 109-110.

Thus, in the simple comparative sentence "*Päikäl dengizdek keng*" (N. Yakubov), "The field is wide like the sea," an enthimema is expressed. The well-known part (the statement, "The sea is wide") is not expressed in this enthimema, but it is fully implied. One can conclude that in simple comparative sentences, two statements, as it were combined and crossed, compose a single unified, complex (trinomial) statement.

According to the logical foundation the semantic structure of simple comparative sentences always becomes complex; that is, there are present at least two semantic propositions which are connected with each other by a comparative relation.

Here it is necessary to define directly the constituent components of comparative constructions, interpreting them both syntactically and semantically. According to S. L. Neveleva, already in ancient Indian poetical and grammatical treatises, beginning with Panini, the quadrinomial composition of the comparison is emphasized.[4] Some linguists note trinomial composition of the comparison; for example, M. I. Cheremisina offers such a formula {A [β (B)]}, for comparative constructions in Russian; the basis of comparison is not taken into consideration in this formula.[5] Using this formula for comparative sentences in Uzbek, it is possible to propose the formula {A [(B) β] C}, where shaped brackets denote that the expression is in the sentence form, A is a symbol of a subject of comparison, B is a symbol of a standard of comparison, β is a formal indicator of the comparative relation, and C is a symbol of the basis of comparison. Compare: "*qavun äsäldäy shirin*," "The melon is as sweet as honey;" "*qavun äsäldän shirin*," "The melon is more sweet, than honey. In these sentences *qavun* is A; *äsäl* is B; *shirin* is C; *-däy* and *-dän* are β. It is necessary to note that the character of the comparison is not always the same. There are two types of comparison: 1) comparison based on similarity, or comparative-identifying comparison, as illustrated by the first sentence; 2) comparison based on difference, or

[4] S. L. Neveleva, *Voprosy poètiki drevne-indiiskogo èposa* (Moscow, 1979), p. 38.

[5] M. I. Cheremisina, *Sravnitel'nye konstruktsii russkogo iazyka* (Novosibirsk, 1976), pp. 17-18.

comparative-distinguishing comparison, as illustrated by the second sentence.

Thus, in comparative-identifying sentences the form *-däy/-dek* (or its equivalents such as *käbi*, *singäri*, etc.) stand for the formal indicator (β), while for comparative-distinguishing sentences, it is the form *-dän* (or sometimes its equivalents: *-gä qärägändä*, *-gä nisbätän*, etc.) that stands for the formal indicator (β). However, many linguists consider the form *-raq* to be a formal indicator in the latter case. This form creates the comparative degree of the adjective.[6] As a matter of fact, as is the case in all other Turkic languages, there is no comparative degree of the adjective in Uzbek,[7] and the affix *-raq* does not itself indicate comparison, but rather indicates that the quality expressed by the adjective (or adverb) to which this affix is added, is weak or substandard. For this reason Prof. Hojiev points to the presence of the diminutive degree (*azäytirmä däräjä*) and notes that the *-raq* affix is a formal indicator of this degree.[8] In the Uzbek language, as in all other Turkic languages, the relationship of the distinguishing comparison is expressed by a construction with the ablative case (less often by separate postpositions), and for this reason it is proper to regard the form of the ablative case *-dän* as the formal indicator in such instances.

In both types of comparative sentences, the interaction and relation of semantic propositions are realized by the relation of comparativization. But only one of these propositions is fully expressed explicitly in the syntactic structure, while the othere finds its explicit expression only partially. In the sentence *qavun äsälday shirin* (*qavun äsäldän shirin*), one proposition is fully expressed explicitly in

[6] See, for example, U. Tursunov, J. Mukhtarov, and Sh. Rähmätulläev, *Hazirgi ozbek ädäbiy tili* (Tashkent, 1975), p. 152; N. Z. Zufarova, *Stepeni sravneniia i sravnitel'nye konstruktsii v sovremennom angliiskom i uzbekskom iazykakh* (AKD, Tashkent, 1971), p. 14.

[7] See Sh. Shaäbduräḥmanov, M. Askarova, Ä. Hajiev and others, *Hazirgi ozbek ädäbiy tili*, I qism (Tashkent, 1980), p. 254; A. I. Vasil'ev, "Sposoby vyrazheniia sravneniia v iakutskom iazyke," in *Narody i iazyki Sibiri* (Novosibirsk, 1980), p. 63.

[8] Shaäbduräḥmanov *et al.*, *Hazirgi ozbek ädäbiy tili*, p. 255.

the part *qavun shirin*, but in the part *äsäldäy* quite another proposition is expressed in abbreviated form (namely "*äsäl shirin*," "honey is sweet"). These two propositions have common predicates (qualities), and because of the predicates' identity, the expression of one of them is omitted in the syntactic structure, facilitating the simplification of the structure. The subjects of these propositions stand for direct elements in the comparison, although the propositions are in a comparative relation with each other.

Now the next question arises: are there any interactions of syntactic positions, and how do they interact, in the two types of simple comparative sentences mentioned above? As was noted earlier, comparison includes three semantic components (a fourth is the formal component). In the structure of the sentence these components are expressed in separate syntactic positions; that is, a specific syntactic position should correspond to each semantic component, and consequently the primary determinative positional structure of both types of simple comparative sentence consists of three syntactic positions (or sometimes of four). But the positional structure of sentences of this type depends on the character of the comparison; and for this reason it is important to examine these two types of simple comparative sentences separately.

Comparative-identifying sentences: In this type of sentence the basis for comparison may be a static or dynamic quality; that is, it may be expressed by an adjective (or some other nominal part of speech), or by a verb. Compare: (1) "*Qädähläri yaqutdäy parlaq*" (Aibek), "The goblets are radiant like a ruby." (2) "*Näzirpalvan khuddi godäk balädek hongräb yubardi*" (O. Umarbekov), "Nazirpalvan began to cry loudly, like a child."

In case (1), the comparative basis of the sentence is expressed in three syntactic positions, that is to say, the subject of comparison is in the position of the grammatical subject (*qädähläri*), the standard of comparison is in the position of an adverbial modifier (*yaqutdäy*), and the basis of comparison is in the position of a predicate (*parlaq*). One can say that the distribution and interaction of syntactic positions are constant in this case. A position model of the sentence is "Subject + Adverbial Modifier + Predicate." This positional structure may be expanded with other syntactic positions, but this does not affect the comparative basis of the sentence; compare: "*Uning qädähläri bu kun yaqutdäy parlaq*," "His goblets today are radiant like ruby."

It is important to note, that based on the possibility of the implicit expression of basis of comparison in such cases, one may derive a model of the comparative sentence of this type, i.e. "Subject + Predicate." Example: "*Tumän - tämäki tutunidek*" (R. Parfi), "The mist is like tobacco smoke." In this sentence, the basis of the comparison is not expressed explicitly, but it has its own implicit expression in the standard of comparison (*tämäki tutunidek*), which is in the position of a predicate. It is evident that the syntactic structure is simplified to the maximum degree, but the propositions' integrity and their comparative relation do not suffer because of this. The designation of the standard of comparison acquires a predicative meaning and in this way the element of comparison is directly wedged within the process of predication itself, and comparative predication appears in the sentence. This fact ensures a quite close relation among the semantic propositions which make up the sentence's semantic substrate.

In case (2), the comparative basis of the sentence is also expressed in three syntactic positions, i.e. the subject of comparison is in the position of the subject (*Näzirpalvan*), the standard of comparison is in the position of the adverbial modifier (*gudäk balädek*), and the basis of comparison is in the position of a predicate (*hungräb yubardi*). The positional model of the sentence is "Subject + Adverbial Modifier + Predicate." But in this case, the model is not constant, since the concretizer of the quality (the basis of comparison) may also participate and may occupy a separate syntactic position; and this position, more often than not the position of the adverbial modifier, is in direct contact with the predicate, i.e. "Subject + adverbial modifier (replaced by the expression of the standard of comparison) + adverbial modifier 2 (replaced by concretizing expression) + predicate. Example: "*Suv zärräläri khuddi yamğir käbi mäyin šavillärdi*" (F. Musäjanov), "The drops of water softly murmured like raindrops." The formation of such a positional model depends in the first place on the semantics of the verb which acts as the expression of the basis for comparison. If the verb needs no semantic concretization, the second syntactic position of the adverbial modifier participating in the sentence's expression of the basis of comparison does not appear in the comparative sentence. Naturally, the sentence may be expanded by syntactic positions which are not relevant for the basis of comparison.

It must be noted that although the expression of the subject of comparison in the syntactic position of the subject is widespread, it does not preclude the possibility of its expression in other syntactic positions. For example, it may be expressed in the position of a direct object. In this case, it is not the subject, but the object of the semantic proposition that enters into the direct comparative relation. Here there appears semantic parallelism between the positions of the direct object and adverbial modifier, not between the syntactic positions of the subject and adverbial modifier, since the comparative elements are in these positions already. Example: "*U Räjäbni oz färzandidek yäkhshi korädi*" (A. Husäynov), "He likes Rajab like his own son." The positional model is "Subject + direct object + adverbial modifier + Predicate." But the components of the comparison are expressed in three positions, i.e. here the subject is not relevant for the comparative basis of the sentence. It is also interesting to observe that in Uzbek, as in all Turkic languages, the semantic parallelism of the elements of comparison is not accompanied by formal parallelism in such cases;[9] the strict regularity observed in Turkic languages in the order of adding affixes prevents this. If it is essential for the comparative elements to be arranged in identical form, then the repeated secondary predicate which had been eliminated is used: "*U Räjäbni oz färzändini yäkhshi korgändek yäkhshi korädi*," "He likes Rajab as he likes his own son." But in this case a definite surplus of linguistic media is noticeable.

Comparative-distinguishing sentences: In this kind of comparative sentences two cases are observed, i.e. either static or dynamic qualities serve as the basis of comparison. Compare: (1) "*Mehman atädän uluğ*" (proverb), "A guest is more honored than one's father." (2) "*Tulänbai ämäki hämmädän kop gäpirärdi*" (Säid Ähmäd), "Uncle Tulänbai spoke most of all."

In case (1), the subject of comparison is expressed in the position of the subject (*mehman*), the standard of comparison is in the position of an indirect complement (*atädän*), and the basis of comparison is

[9] In other languages, including Russian ("*on liubit Radzhaba, kak svoego syna*," with both elements of comparison in the genitive case) and Spanish (cf. A. V. Suprun, *Grammatika i semantika prostogo predlozheniia (na materiale ispanskogo iazyka* [Moscow, 1977], p. 216), such parallelism is observed fully.

expressed in the position of the predicate; that is, the basis of comparison is expressed in three syntactic positions. The permanent positional model of the comparative sentence of this case is: "Subject + indirect complement + predicate," and precisely these positions are relevant for the basis of comparison.

As was noted, in the comparative-identifying sentences of the first case, both explicit and implicit expression of the basis of comparison is possible. This is explained by the fact that the degree to which the quality underlying the basis of comparison is related to the elements of comparison is identical, and for this reason the standard of comparison may imply the basis of comparison as well; but it is absolutely impossible to express implicitly the basis of comparison in comparative-distinguishing sentences, since in these the degree of relatedness of the quality which underlies the basis of the comparison to the elements of the comparison is *not* identical, but quite different, and indeed the aim of the sentence is to show this difference. Therefore the standard of comparison logically cannot imply the basis of comparison.

In the type of sentences under consideration, the subject of comparison may be expressed not only in the position of the subject, but in the position of an adverbial modifier and of an object; that is, it is possible to include the subject, circumstances, and objects of the semantic positions into the direct comparative relation. Compare: "*Qishlaq khojälik mähsulatläri shähärgä qärägändä qishlaqdä ärzanraq*" (from the newspaper *Qishlaq häqiqäti*), "The agricultural goods are cheaper in the village than in town;" the positional model is "Subject + indirect object + adverbial modifier + predicate." "*Bu kitab sendän korä mengä zärurraq*" (A. Juraev), "I need this book more than you do;" the positional model is "Subject + indirect object + indirect object + predicate." In both models, the position of the subject is not relevant for the comparative basis of the sentence.

In case (2), the designation of the subject of comparison (*Tulänbai ämäki*) is in the syntactic position of the subject, and the designation of the basis of comparison (*gäpirärdi*) is in the position of the predicate. But the expression of the standard of comparison (*hämmädän*) does not occupy a separate syntactic position. In the comparative sentences of this type, the role of concretizing words is of great importance; in the above sentence the word *kop* acts as the concretizer. The degree of difference in the relationship between the quality (that is, of the basis of comparison) and the elements of comparison is indicated by this concretizing word. For this reason the word-form which expresses the standard of comparison is included into the syntactic position occupied by the concretizer; it is in direct grammatical connection with this word only, not with the predicate. Generally concretizer occupies the position of an adverbial modifier, meaning that in our sentence the standard of comparison, together with the concretizer, occupies the position of an adverbial modifier of measure and degree. The positional comparative model is "Subject + adverbial modifier + predicate." The expansion of this model by other syntactic positions does not influence the comparative basis of the sentence.

As is evident, simple comparative sentences display a characteristic semantic-syntactic mechanism. In the two types of the simple comparative sentences discussed above and in their subtypes, the action of this mechanism is manifested distinctively, and in each type the peculiar interaction of the elements of meaning and semantics require a specific, corresponding interaction of the elements of syntactic structure. It must be noted that this mechanism is yet more complex in simple sentences featuring comparative constructions which express the components of comparison in reverse order, according to the formula "[(B) β] C A." Such distinctive simple comparative sentences are widespread in Uzbek. The comparative relation turns to be complementary in them; that is, the expression of the comparative relation does not directly enter into the grammatical frame of the sentence. Naturally, such sentences require separate consideration, and their semantic- syntactic mechanisms should be the objects of another investigation.

One may conclude that in the simple comparative sentences a complicated semantic substrate is always expressed. Minimally, this substrate consists of two semantic propositions, connected by a comparative relation, depending upon the distinctive semantic-syntactic mechanism of a given sentence. This mechanism noticeably enlarges the semantic volume of sentences which from the the structural and formal perspective are simple sentences; and in this connection one may speak of the asymmetry of semantic and syntactic structures. The characteristic feature of simple comparative sentences is the presence of a semantic-syntactic asymmetry whose regularities lie in the mechanisms named above; such asymmetry provides the informational saturation of structurally simple sentences. Consequently the peculiar semantic-syntactic mechanism of the simple comparative sentence demonstrates one form of the manifestation of an important tendency of language, namely the tendency toward linguistic economy.

THE LATIN SOURCES FOR KHWAREZM

Ruth I. Meserve

Introductory Remarks

Soviet archaeological finds in this century relevant to prehistoric Khwarezm and to ancient pre-Islamic Khwarezm as well as to medieval Khwarezm have provided the most important and extensive evidence toward a more complete history of Khwarezm.[1] With its comparative isolation from the rest of Central Asia, Khwarezm not only maintained important ties to the north with the Volga basin and to the south with Khorasan, but was also the center of a great empire at the time of the Khwarezm Shahs prior to the Mongol conquest. The fact that Khwarezm looked less toward the Latin and Greek west or the Chinese east has caused most scholars to somewhat neglect both the Chinese sources[2] and, particularly, the Latin materials recorded by members of religious orders, historians, and geographers from the West. Yet Khwarezm does appear in Latin sources, which should be examined if only because they yield tiny pieces of information, useful to the overall history of medieval Khwarezm.

Research into the extensive Latin corpus for materials on medieval Khwarezm has been greatly aided by:

1. Pentti Aalto and Tuomo Pekkanen, *Latin Sources on North-Eastern Eurasia*, I-II, (Wiesbaden: Otto Harrassowitz, 1975, 1980). [hereafter designated A-P]
2. Ligeti Lajos, "A magyar nyelv török kapcsolatai és ami körülöttük van," *Magyar nyelv* LXXII (1976): 11-27. [hereafter designated L]

[1] Many Soviet scholars have contributed considerably to the study of Khwarezm: Tolstov, Itina, Masson, Nerazik, Vorobyeva, D'iakanov, Trofimova, Vainberg. See also, B. Spuler, "Chwarizms (Choresmiens) Kultur nach S. P. Tolstovs Forschungen," *Historia*, I/4 (1950), pp. 601-615; this study has been reprinted in Spuler, *Gesammelte Aufsätze*, (Leiden: E. J. Brill, 1980), pp. 150-164.

[2] Since the work by Pelliot ("Le nom du Xwarizm dans les textes chinois," *T'oung Pao*, 34 (1938), pp. 146-152) on the Chinese name of Khwarezm, this gap is being filled in by such recent work as that by I. P. Petrushevskii, N. N. Vakturskaia, Hajji Yusuf Chang, etc.

3. *Glossar zur frühmittelalterlichen Geschichte im östlichen Europa. Serie A: Lateinische Namen bis 900, Band III, Lieferung 4, Constantinus V. - Crocco*, herausgegeben von Frank Kämpfer und Klaus Zernack, (Stuttgart: Franz Steiner Verlag Wiesbaden GmbH, 1986). [hereafter designated G]

For the purposes of this paper, it should be noted that only the term Chorasmi (and its variants: Chorasmius, Corasmi, Carasmi, Chorosmenia, Korosmina, etc.) has been used;[3] other place names such as Urgandj, Gurdandj, and, perhaps, even the Oxus [Amu Darya], the Gihon, and the Aral Sea should all be searched for in the extensive Latin corpus in order to present a more complete view of medieval Khwarezm.

The material found in the Latin sources on Khwarezm can be broken down, roughly, into three large categories: geographical, mythical or epic, and historical evidence. The examples given here, within these three categories, are by no means complete, specifically in terms of late medieval Latin texts, where much work remains to be done by those interested in the Khwarezmians and their role in the Latin Kingdom during the period of the later Crusades.

I. *Geographical Notices in the Latin Corpus*

A fair number of early medieval Latin texts made mention of Khwarezm in relation to other countries such as Sogdiana, Parthia, and/or Bactria; it should be noted, however, that many drew upon original Greek sources dealing with the campaigns and conquests of Alexander the Great (356-323 B.C.). For these early geographical notices see, for example:

[3] Care must be taken to distinguish a very similar place name that appears in medieval Latin texts, that of Chorazin (Chorazim, Corocaym) which was one of the ten cities of the Decapolis mentioned in Matthew XI.21 and Luke X.13. See, for example, *Paulys Real-encyclopädie der classischen Altertumswissenschaft* (Stuttgart: J. B. Metzlerscher Verlag, 1899), III, columns 2406-2407; William Smith, ed., *A Dictionary of Greek and Roman Geography*, I-II, (London: John Murray, 1878), I, p. 613.

A. On Sogdiana and the Oxus:
1. Rufus Festus Avienus (mid-4th C. A.D.) [A-P, G]

B. In lists with the Dahae and Sacae:
1. *Itinerarium Alexandri ad Constantium Augustum* (341-345 A.D.) [A-P]
2. Quintus Curtius Rufus (age of Claudius, fl. 400 A.D.) [A-P]
3. Paulus Orosius (c. 5th C. A.D.) [A-P]
4. Fabius Planciades Fulgentius Afer (5th-6th C. A.D.) [A-P]
5. M. Iunianus Iustinus (3rd C. A.D.) [A-P]

C. In lists mentioning the people of Scythia, Seres, Anartacae:
1. Iulius Honorius (fl. 5th C. A.D.) [A-P, G]

D. In lists with Gandari, Paricani, Arsi, etc.:
1. C. Plinius Secundus (62-c.114 A.D.) [A-P]

E. In lists with Parthia:
1. *Ravennatis anonymi cosmographiae Graecae versio vetustior* (9th C. from Greek 7th C.) [A-P, G]

F. In lists with Scythia, Geloni, Massagetae, etc.
1. *Cosmographia olim Aethici dicta* (6th C. A.D.) [A-P]

Very little information is offered in these Latin texts about the region of Khwarezm or the people inhabiting it; the name simply appears in lists of countries or peoples. There are some exceptions though, where, for example, in Quintus Curtius Rufus the name of a Khwarezmian satrap (Phrataphernes)[4] at the time of Alexander is given.

II. *Mythical or Epic Sources*

Aalto and Pekkanen, though more complete on the early medieval Latin texts than the *Glossar*, do not list the Hungarian Latin

[4] [Quintus Curtius Rufus], *History of Alexander*, VIII. i. 8, translated by John C. Rolfe, (London: Heinemann, 1946), II, pp. 234-235.

texts that do appear in the *Glossar*. As already noted by Ligeti, these Hungarian Latin texts that mention Khwarezm, do so in the capacity of relating a Hungarian "epic" version of the story of the Huns.[5] All four texts present basically the same story of a Hun-Khwarezmian marriage alliance. Three parallel passages - indicated as [a], [b], and [c] - from the four Hungarian texts are presented for comparison in the Appendix.

Of the four Hungarian Latin texts on Khwarezm, the *Chronicon pictum Vindobonense* (14th century) can be considered the most complete; the text of Simon de Kéza (fl. 1290) omitted the more fanciful description of the rather inhospitable zone with its serpents, poisonous animals, tigers, and unicorns in the first passage [a] as well as mention of Bendekuz, father of Attila, in section [b]. Both the *Chronici Budensis e codice Sambuci* (14th century) and the *Chronicon Posoniense* (14th century) were abbreviated in their versions of the third excerpt [c] and neither made any reference to Khwarezm at this point in the text.

III. *Historical Sources*

Many of the later medieval Latin texts covered two major, historical events of the thirteenth century: a) the Mongol attack on Khwarezm, beginning in 1219 and ending with the flight of the Khwarezmians toward the west; and b) the involvement of Khwarezmian soldiers, in alliance with the Ayyubid sultan of Egypt, in the sack of Tiberias, Nablus, and eventually Jerusalem in the year 1244. And it is the events of 1244 that dominated by far the Latin texts on Khwarezm and the Khwarezmians. The Latin texts that covered these events - not listed in the *Glossar* because of the cut off date of 900 A.D., nor in Aalto and Pekkanen - deserve, perhaps, more attention. Some are used, for example, but not translated, in *A History of the Crusades, Volume Two: The Later Crusades 1189-1311* edited by Robert Lee Wolff and Harry W. Hazard under the general editorship of Kenneth M. Setton (Madison, Wisconsin: University of Wisconsin Press, 1969). When these texts have been translated, either fully or in part, the materials for Khwarezm have not been assimilated,

[5] Ligeti, p. 25.

primarily because the scholars were more interested in textual philology or western medieval and Crusader history than in those involved on the other side of the dispute over the Holy Land. There is, of course, a strong bias in favor of the Crusaders and Christianity in these Latin chronicles, letters, travel 'diaries', etc.

A. *The Mongol Attack on Khwarezm Beginning in 1219*

Most of the Latin texts simply noted the destruction of Khwarezm, presenting none of the details of the Mongol attack. This is true, for example, of such accounts as that of Matthew Paris (1200-1259) in his *Chronica majora*,[6] in the *Chronicon de Mailros* (13th century),[7] or that by Frater Ricoldo da Monte Croce (d. 1309).[8] One major exception to this is the description given by Simon de Saint-Quentin (13th century), that has been preserved in Vincent of Beauvais (d. 1264), *Speculum historiale*.[9] Simon, a Minorite, accompanied Ascelinus in 1245 on his papal mission to the Mongols as directed by Innocent IV and the Council of Lyons. The following episode is from the critical edition of Simon de Saint-Quentin made by Jean Richard.[10]

[6] [Matthew Paris] Matthaei Parisiensis, Monachi Sancti Albani, *Chronica majora*, edited by Henry Richards Luard in *Rerum britannicarum medii aevi scriptores* [Rolls Series], No. 37, Vol. IV, p. 299. For an English version of this passage see, Matthew Paris's *English History from the year 1235 to 1273*, I-III, translated by the Rev. J. A. Giles, (London: George Bell and Sons, 1889), II, p. 491.

[7] *The Chronicle of Melrose from the Cottonian Manuscript, Faustina B. IX in the British Museum: A complete and full-sized facsimile in collotype*, with an introduction by Alan Orr Anderson and Marjorie Ogilvie Anderson, and an index by William Croft Dickinson, (London: Percy Lund Humphries & Co., Ltd., 1936), p. 92.

[8] J. C. M. Laurent, *Peregrinatores medii ævi quator*, (Leipzig, 1873), p. 120.

[9] [Vincent of Beauvais] Vincentius Bellovacensis, *Speculum quadruplex sive speculum maius: naturale, doctrinale, morale, historiale*, I-IV (Graz: Akademische Druck-u.Verlagsanstalt, 1965), IV. *Speculum historiale*, Book 30, chapter 88, p. 1215.

[10] [Simon de Saint-Quentin], *Histoire des Tartares*, Documents Relatifs à l'Histoire des Croisades publiés par l'Académie des Inscriptions et Belles-Lettres, VIII, edited by Jean Richard (Paris: Librairie Orientaliste Paul Geuthner, 1965), p. 53.

XXX, 88. - Qualiter Corasminos destruentes fugaverunt

Itaque post victoriam de Indis, ut predictum est, erigentes cervicem superbie ac de totius mundi subjectione presumentes, ad Corasminos trans miserunt primos nuncios tanquam ad sibi propinquiores, arroganter eis mandantes quatinus Cingiscam et ejus exercitui humiliter obedirent eique servicium perpetuum cum tributo impenderent. At vero Corasmini super mandacione sibi facta quamplurimum indignati predictos nuncios omnes fecerunt interfici. Tartari ergo super illorum occasione supra modum indignati et turbati, et congregata multitudine magna Tartarorum eorumque qui eis voluntarii vel inviti se conjunxerant terram Corasminorum invaserunt, quotquot invenire potuerunt ex eis gladio prosternentes omnesque alios tanquam exules et profugos de finibus illis penitus effugantes.

I offer here the following translation of this passage:

XXX, 88. How they put to flight the murderous (lit. "destroying") Khwarezmians:

And so after the victory over the Indians, as was told earlier, and rising up in haughty boldness and anticipating the subjugation of the entire world, they [the Mongols] sent over to the Khwarezmians (their) first ambassadors as they drew near to them, arrogantly ordering them on how to humbly obey Chinggis khan and his army by giving perpetual service to him along with tribute. But, indeed, the Khwarezmians, being very indignant concerning this order given to them, caused all the earlier mentioned ambassadors to be killed. The Tartars [i.e. the Mongols], therefore, over the massacre of those (ambassadors) and over (their) great indignation and anger, and when a great multitude of Tartars had

> been gathered together and a mob of those who had joined them voluntarily or rather (of those whom) they had invited to join them, they invaded the land of Khwarezm, dispatching as many as they were able to find by the sword and driving all others completely from that land as exiles and fugitives.

Richard considered this episode "somewhat deformed" ("quelque peu déformé"), denying the demand for tribute and citing only the version of al-Nasawī on the Mongol attack on Khwarezm.[11] Mongol chronicles,[12] however, bear out a good deal of what Simon de Saint-Quentin says and, hence, the importance of looking at Latin sources, where in the past the overwhelming tendency has been to consult primarily the materials in Arabic and/or Persian for this period of history.

B. *The Khwarezmian Soldiers and the Sack of Jerusalem in 1244*

The details of the events leading up to and including the sack of Jerusalem, though abbreviated compared to some of the other chronicles that are mentioned below, are continued in Simon de Saint-Quentin's account.[13]

> Itaque Corasmini persecucionem eorum declinantes fugerunt et in fines se Persidis maximeque in civitatem Georgie Trifelis effuderunt, ubi

[11] Simon de Saint-Quentin, Richard edition, p. 53.

[12] Hans-Rainer Kämpfe, *Das Asaraγči-neretü-yin teüke des Byamba erke dai»cwing alias Šamba Jasaγ (Eine mongolische Chronik des 17. Jahrhunderts)* (Wiesbaden: Otto Harrassowitz, 1983), p. 72. See also the present author's article, "The Right of Safe Conduct: A Re-examination of the Cause for the Mongol Assault on Khwarezm, 1219-1225," in *Fifth International Congress of Mongolists*, ed. Sh. Bira (Ulaanbaatar: International Association for Mongol Studies, 1992), vol. 3, pp. 232-240.

[13] Simon de Saint-Quentin, Richard edition, pp. 53-54.

etiam .vii. millia hominum occiderunt. Postmodum vero cum in fines illos Tartari supervenerunt, iterum Corasmini fugientes ad tempus in terra soldani Turquie latuerunt. Postea vero a soldano Babilonie domino Egipti invitati atque conducti in regnum Hierosolimitanum venientes et Christianos debellantes ante Gazam civitatem magnam Francorum multitudinem Domino permittente prostraverunt et gloriosum Domini nostri sepulcrum destruxerunt atque intra et extra sanctam civitatem Christianos quamplurimos occiderunt, quod factum est anno Domini MCCXLIII <sicut infra dicetur in loco sua>. Qui scilicet Corasmini, postquam Deo permittente tantum facinus et impietatem commiserunt, tandem ipso Domino disponente jam fere omnes ad nichilum redacti sunt.

Translation

And so the Khwarezmians have fled persecution avoiding them [the Tartars] and have poured forth to the borders of Persia itself [and] especially toward Tiflis in Georgia where, also, they have killed 7000 men. Soon after, indeed, when the Tartars appeared unexpectedly in those places, again the fleeing Khwarezmians concealed [themselves] in due time in the land of the Sultan of Turkey. After that, indeed invited and gathered together by the Sultan of Babylon lord of Egypt, those coming into the kingdom of Jerusalem and subduing the Christians before the city of Gaza have destroyed a great multitude of Franks, who surrendered themselves unto the Lord, and have torn down the holy sepulcre of our Lord; and so, within and without the sacred city they have killed as many Christians as possible in the year of the Lord 1244 <as told later in the place itself>. No doubt the Khwarezmians who have, after [being] let loose by God, committed so

> many misdeeds and irreverences, finally, by the Lord himself disposing of nearly all, they have been driven back into nothingness.

These events are also mentioned, though only slightly, in Frater Ricoldo da Monte Croce.[14] A brief description of the siege and fall of Jerusalem (23 August 1244) can be found in the *Annals of Waverly* from the Cistercian abbey of Waverly near Farnham in Surrey, England.[15] The *Annals* covered the period from 1128 to 1291. More detail on the invasion of Jerusalem, the defense by the knights Templar and Hospitallers, and the destruction of the Church of the Holy Sepulcre, can be found in the *Guillelmi de Nangiaco chronicon*,[16] written by Guillaume de Nangio (d. 1300), a Benedictine archivist and chronicler from St. Deny. In the *Chronica Buriensis* (1212-1301) from Bury St. Edmunds Abbey, the following passage gives a very brief description of events that would be elaborated upon by others.

> An amazing battle was fought near Gaza between the Christians and Khorazmians on the vigil of the feast of St. Lucy (i.e. 12 December 1944); the Khorazmians exterminated the complete army of the kingdom of Syria together with numerous Christians.[17]

Information on the battle of Gaza (17 October 1244) can also be found in the *Annals of Burton* from the abbey of Burton-upon-Trent in

[14] Laurent, p. 120.

[15] Henry Richards Luard, ed., *Annales monasterii de Waverleia (A.D. 1-1291)*, in *Annales monastici*, II, Rolls Series, no. 36, vol. 2, (London, 1865), pp. 334-335.

[16] *Guillemi de Nangiaco chroniconò* in *Recueil des historiens des Gaules et de la France*, XX (1840): 550.

[17] Antonia Gransden, ed., *The Chronicle of Bury St. Edmunds 1212-1301* (London: Nelson, 1964), p. 13.

Staffordshire, England.[18] The *Annals of Burton* begin with the founding of the abbey in 1004 and conclude with the year 1263.

The size of the Khwarezmian force that came into Jerusalem has been set at varying figures by medieval chroniclers. Matthew Paris, for example, simply recorded, according to one source, that "several thousand armed knights" came; another source he cited referred to "a countless multitude".[19] Their number was put at 21,000 horsemen by the *Chronicon de Mailros*, the principal monastic chronicle of Scotland from the Cistercian monastery of Melrose.[20] This larger figure is agreed upon by Marino Sanudo called Torsello (c. 1270- c. 1343), who presented two copies of his *Liber secretorum fidelium crucis* to Pope John XXII on 24 September 1321 and another copy to Charles IV of France in 1323.[21] A Venetian patrician, Sanudo had been in the Latin Kingdom of Jerusalem in the 1280's, where he was actively involved in the family's commercial interests. Greatly concerned with how to regain the Holy Land after the fall of Acre to the Mamluks in 1291, Sanudo's book specifically contested that the Holy Land could be retaken and contained not only the plans for this venture but also how the Holy Land should then be governed by the Crusaders after their successful reconquest of the region. But more important to this study, the volume also contained a history of the Holy Land up to the year 1301.[22] Under the year 1244, when the Khwarezmians appeared on the scene, Sanudo told of the arrival of their cavalry and estimated the force at 20,000 men.[23]

[18] Henry Richards Luard, ed., *Annales de Burton (A.D. 1004-1263)* in *Annales monastici* I, Rolls Series, no. 36, vol. 1, (London, 1864), p. 258.

[19] In the Giles translation of Matthew Paris see Vol. II, pp. 523, 498.

[20] *The Chronicle of Melrose*, pp. 92-95.

[21] [Marino Sanudo Torsello] Marinus Sanutus dictus Torsellus, *Liber secretorum fidelium crucis super Terrae Sanctae recuperatione et conservatione quo et Terrae Sanctae historia ab origine & eiusdem vicinarumque provinciarum geographica descriptio continetur*, (Toronto: University of Toronto Press, 1972), p. vii.

[22] *Ibid.*, see the Foreword by Joshua Prawer, especially pages viii, xiii-xiv.

[23] *Ibid.*, p. 217.

Extensive material on the events leading up to the sack of Jerusalem and the final disappearance of the Khwarezmian soldiers may be found in the *Chronicon de Mailros.*[24] In this thirteenth century chronicle, written over a period of one hundred years and recorded by numerous hands, there are a number of letters that have been inserted which have direct bearing on the Khwarezmian soldiers in the Holy Land:

1. Robert, the patriarch of Jerusalem
2. Queen of Cyprus
3. Archbishop of Tyre
4. Bishops of Acre, Sidon, Lydda
5. Hermann of Périgord, master of the Knights of the Temple
6. William, master of the house of the Hospital of St. John
7. the preceptor of the house of St. Mary of the Teutonic Knights
8. Odo de Montbéliard, lord of Tiberias and constable of the Kingdom of Jerusalem
9. Philip de Montfort, lord of Teron

Most of these letters were sent to pope Innocent IV, reporting the disasters in the Holy Land.

In a similar vein, Matthew Paris' *Chronica majora* also records, both in prose narrative and in the use of imbedded letters, the events leading to the sack of Jerusalem.

> . . . certain extremely cruel and inhuman men who dwell on the confines of the Red Sea, and who are for the most part subject to the sultan of Babylon, and called Choermians, fled from the threatening storm, by avoiding the irruptions of the Tartars; and they went to the sultan of Babylon, and demanded hastily and insolently a place wherein to dwell. When the sultan found out that if he should arrogantly deny their requests, they would forcibly take what they wanted at the edge of the

[24] *The Chronicle of Melrose*, pp. 92-95.

> sword, he said to them: "At no great distance from this place there are some people whom we call Christians, they inhabit maritime places, they scorn our laws, and are troublesome and annoying to us, and threaten to become still more so; their most important place of resort is Jerusalem. Go therefore boldly, cast them out, and live where they now do. Which, when you have obtained, you will be enriched with precious spoils, and will have opulent lands, and rejoice in castles and cities to your hearts' desire, and can, from that time, be happy in my patronage, and in the patronage of all my people." Whereupon they, elated with these words, first attack Jerusalem, and massacre a large number of Christians, as we are now more fully informed in the letter from the nobles of that land.[25]

Some of the material is the same as that found in the *Chronicon de Mailros*, though sometimes in greater detail. The letter of the prelates sent from Acre on 25 November 1244 to the prelates of England and France also concerned the invasion of the Khwarezmians in 1244. This letter, for example, related that the Khwarezmians came with their wives and children and that the armed men numbered several thousand.[26] William (de Chateau Neuf), master of the Hospitallers, wrote on the daily assaults and tactics of the Khwarezmians on Jerusalem, driving many to flee at night, who then

> . . . wandered about in the trackless and desert parts of the mountains, till they at length came to a narrow pass, and there they fell into an ambuscade of the enemy, who, surrounding them on all sides, attacked them with swords, arrows, stones, and other weapons, slew and cut to pieces, according to

[25] See the Giles translation of Matthew Paris, II. p. 491; for the Latin text, see the Luard edition, IV, pp. 299-300.

[26] Matthew Paris, Giles translation, II, p. 523; Luard edition, IV, p. 338.

> a correct computation, about seven thousand men and women, and caused such a massacre, that the blood of those of the faith, with sorrow I say it, ran down the sides of the mountains like water. Young men and virgins they hurried off with them into captivity, and retired into the holy city, where they cut the throats, as of sheep doomed to the slaughter, of the nuns, and aged and infirm men, who, had fled to the church of the Holy Sepulchre and to Calvary, a place consecrated by the blood of our Lord, thus perpetrating in this holy sanctuary such a crime as the eyes of men had never seen since the commencement of the world.[27]

Also included in the *Chronica majora* is a lengthy letter of Frederick II (HRE) to Richard of Cornwall on the sack of Jerusalem.[28] Details are given on how successfully the Khwarezmian army battled the Christians; a list is given of those who escaped from being slain or made prisoner.[29]

The end of the Khwarezmians is dealt with less than the previous events. Although the Latin kingdom endured repeated attacks from the Khwarezmian forces and their supporters, by the year 1246 internal disputes between the Khwarezmians and the various Ayyubid sultans had surfaced. Because the sultan al-Malik al-Salih Najm al-Din Ayyub (in Egypt) had not fulfilled his promises, the Khwarezmians changed their allegiance to sultan al-Malik al-Salih Isma'il (in Damascus), who gave a daughter in marriage to the Khwarezmian leader. In the ensuing internecine battles of the Ayyubids, the Khwarezmians suffered near annihilation near Baalbek from the combined forces of the sultan al-Mansur Ibrahim (Homs) and an-Nasir Yusuf (Aleppo), both of whom were supported by the sultan of

[27]Matthew Paris, Giles translation, II, p. 499; Luard edition, IV, pp. 307 ff.

[28] Matthew Paris, Giles translation, II, pp. 491-496; Luard edition, IV, p. 300 ff.

[29] Matthew Paris, Giles translation, II, pp. 497-500; Luard edition, IV, pp. 434 ff.

Egypt. Those Khwarezmians who survived fled back to the East. Much of this information has been recorded in Matthew Paris' *Chronica majora*. There is, for example, an account of their end from the Bishop of Tortosa.[30] Divine intervention to rid the Holy Land from the continued threat of the Khwarezmians was also mentioned by some. As has already been noted, Simon de Saint-Quentin made a brief comment on this as did Guy, a knight to the bishop of Chartres. Speaking of God, Guy wrote: "It is he who has purged the Holy Land from the wicked Charismians. He has destroyed them and caused them to disappear entirely from under heaven."[31]

A defeated army, fleeing with refugees and seeking asylum elsewhere, has often presented serious problems to rulers and peoples not involved in the original conflict. Much of Inner Asian history, in fact, has replayed over and over this movement of peoples, shoving and pushing against new neighbors, fighting for a new place to live where they can maintain their own civilization without hindrance from others. The Latin sources on Khwarezm, though extremely limited when compared to the Arabic and Persian materials and strongly biased toward Christian Europe, provide a dramatic view of this process along with the resulting prejudices and fears. These materials reveal another point of view to the overall picture of medieval Khwarezm and its wider role in the history and political problems of the medieval world.

Appendix: The Hungarian Latin Texts on Khwarezm

For editions of these texts and variants to the passages given below see: Emericus Szentpétery, *Scriptores rerum hungaricarum tempore ducum regumque stirpis Arpadianae gestarum* (Budapest: Academia Litter. Hungarica atque Societate Histor. Hungarica, 1937), in 2 volumes; and Albinus Franciscus Gombos, *Catalogus fontium historiae hungaricae aevo ducum et regum ex stirpe Arpad descendentium ab anno christi DCCC usque ad annum MCCCI ab*

[30] Matthew Paris, Luard edition, V, p. 72; VI, p. 116.

[31] "Letters of the Crusaders Written from the Holy Land," *Translations and Reprints from the Original Sources of European History*, I, 4 (no date): 38.

Academia Litterarum de Sancto Stephano rege nominata editus (Budapest, 1937-1943), in 4 volumes.

Chronici Hungarici Compositio Saeculi XIV

S	V
(Chronici Budensis e codice Sambuci)	(Chronicon pictum Vindobonense)

[a] Ex plaga autem estivali subsolari (sic) gens iacet Corosmina et Ethyopia, que Minor India dicitur. Et post hec inter meridiem et cursum Don fluvii est desertum inmeabile, ubi propter intemperiem aeris illius zone sunt serpentes diversi generis, rane velud porci, basillicus (sic) et plura animalia toxicata, tigris et unicornis ibi generantur.

[b] Hic autem in Scythiam, paternam scilicet sedem adiendo uxorem de Scytia non accepit, sed traduxit de Corosmenia de consilio Bendekuz avi sui, quem sanum sed nimis decrepitum dicitur invenisse.

[c] (S has an abbreviated version corresponding to V but there is no mention of Khwarezm)	(V) Iste igitur Chaba filius Atyle est legittimus ex filia Honorii imperatoris Grecorum genitus, cui Edemen et Ed filii sui sunt vocati. Edemen autem cum Ungari in Pannoniam secundario sunt reversi, cum maxima familia patris sui et matris introivit. Nam mater eius de Corosmenis orta erat. Ex isto enim Chaba generatio Abe est egressa. Cum igitur Chaba adiens in Scithiam nobilitate genitricis in communi se iactarent (sic) Hunorum nobilitas ipsum contempnebat asserentes eum non verum esse alumpnum regni Scitie, sed quasi missitalium extere nationis, propter quod ex Scytia uxorem non accepit, sed traduxit de gente Corosmina.

Simon de Kéza

[a] Ex plaga vero estivali subsolana gens iacet Corosmina, Ethiopia eciam, que India minor dicitur, ac post hec inter meridiem et cursum Don fluvii desertum existit immeabile.

[b] omitted

[c] Iste ergo (igitur) Chaba filius Ethele est legitmus ex filia Honorii imperatoris Grecorum genitus, cui Edemen et Ed filii sui sunt vocati. Edemen autem cum Hungari in Pannoniam secundario sunt reversi, cum maxima familia patris (sui) et matris introivit. Nam mater eius de Corosminis orta erat. Ed (Eed) vero in Scithia remansit apud patrem. Ex isto enim Chaba generacio Abe (Aba) est egressa. Cum ergo (igitur) Chaba adiens in Scithiam nobilitate genitricis in communi se iactaret, Hunorum nobilitas ipsum contempnebat, asserentes eum non verum esse alumpnum regni Scithie, sed quasi missitalium extere nacionis. Propter quod uxorum in Scithia (e Scithia) non accepit, sed traduxit de gente Corosmina.

Chronicon Posoniense

[a] Ex plaga vero autem estivali subsolari gens iacet Corosmoia (sic) et Ethiopia, que Minor India dicitur. Et post hoc inter meridiem et cursum Don fluvii est desertum inmeabile, ubi propter intemperiem aeris illius zone sunt serpentes diversi generis, rant ut porci, basilliscus et plura alia animalia toxicata, tigris et unicornus (sic) ibi generantur.

[b] Hic autem in Sciciam adiendo uxorem de Scicia non accepit, sed traduxit de Corosmenia de consilio Wendekuz (sic) avi sunt, quem sanum, sed nimis decrepitum dicitur invenisse.

[c] abbreviated version, but no mention of Khwarezm.

THE PRESUPPOSITIONAL ASPECT

OF THE SIMPLE SENTENCE IN UZBEK

A. Nurmanov

As many researchers have confirmed, the semantic structure of a sentence has a complicated inner structure. It includes not only its propositional, modal, and communicative structures, but its presuppositional structure as well. According to V. Bogdanov, insofar as presupposition represents one of the aspects of the meaning of predicative expressions, it must be reflected in semantic structure.[1] Naturally, each element of the semantic structure of a sentence has its own focus of research, and this is evidenced in the ever increasing interest of linguists in the presuppositional aspect of the sentence.[2]

There is no unified opinion concerning the status of presupposition in linguistic literature. The notion of presupposition (presumption) goes back to the ideas of German scholar G. Frege, who defined it as the natural premise of judgment. Thus, the sentences "Kepler died in poverty / Kepler did not die in poverty" have the identical prerequisite of Kepler's existence. In G. Frege's view the main judgment is often accompanied by other implicit judgments, but as far as presupposition is concerned he deals only with the premise of existence.

E. Keenan proposed distinguishing pragmatic and logical presuppositions. The first is defined by the structure of the individual speaker's thesaurus, while the other is understood as the semantic relation between sentences.[3]

In contemporary linguistics by presupposition is understood either the implicit judgment given in the form of a sentence as the meaning-

[1] V. V. Bogdanov, *Semantiko-sintaksicheskaia organizatsiia predlozheniia* (Leningrad, 1977), p. 139.

[2] A. Nurmanov, "Komakchili konstruktsiialar presuppozitsiyasi," *Ozbek tili vä ädäbiyati*, 1986, No. 6.

[3] E. Keenan, "Two Kinds of Presupposition in Natural Language," in *Studies in Linguistic Semantics*, ed. C. Fillmore and D. Langendven, No. 4 (New York, 1971), pp. 45-52.

ful component of an other explicit thought,[4] or the totality of preliminary (background) knowledge ("the general body of knowledge among interlocutors") which makes a given utterance possible and understandable.[5]

We support the views of those researchers who define presupposition on the basis of the formal structure of the sentence. In particular, D. Lightfoot notes that presuppositions are created "by sentences, not by people," and are determined "by the forms of the sentence, not by the persuasion of this or that speaker."[6]

The concept of presupposition embraces the idea of context (the linguistic environment of a given language unit) and situation (the non-linguistic substratum of a given utterance, the conditions in which the a given utterance occurred).[7] For instance, the sentence "*Bugun instruktorimizni qaldirdim, dädä*" (Äbdulla Qähhar, "*Ujär*"), "Today I defeated the instructor, dad," conveys the intended information only in context. In context, the discussion concerns chess. Thus, this sentence has the presupposition, "*instruktorimiz bilän shäkhmät oynädim*," "I played chess with the instructor." Outside the context the presupposition will be blocked.

Presupposition can be manifested in the lexical meaning of certain words on the basis of people's universal knowledge about the surrounding world and the knowledge of the speakers about the language. For example the sentence "*Men Tashkentdän Moskvagä učdim*," "I flew from Tashkent to Moscow," bears the presupposition, "*samoletda keldim*," "I came by plane;" the lexical meaning of the word *učmaq*, "to fly," along with the general body of knowledge about the language, makes the presupposition understood for inter-

[4] C. Lakoff, "Über generative Semantik," *Semantik und generative Grammatik*, II (Frankfurt am Main, 1972), pp. 308, 355.

[5] G. V. Gak, *Teoreticheskaia grammatika frantsuzskogo iazyka; Sintaksis* (Moscow, 1981), p. 14; N. D. Arutiunova, "Poniatie presuppozitsii v lingvistike," *Izvestiia AN SSSR*, seriia *Literatury i iazyka*, t. 32, vyp. 1 (1973), p. 85.

[6] D. Lightfoot, "Les présuppositions dans la grammaire transformationelle," in *Problèmes de sémantique, Cahier linguistique*, No. 2 (Montréal, 1973), pp. 184, 191.

[7] Gak, *Teoreticheskaia grammatika*, p. 14.

locutors. Again, in the sentence "*Bir qiz keldi*," "A girl came," the presupposition that the girl is unmarried is found in the lexeme *qiz*, "[unmarried] girl."

Moreover, in every language there are special linguistic devices which signal the presence of a presupposition; these may be termed presuppositional signifiers. In modern Uzbek the following particles may serve as presuppositional signifiers: *fäqät*, "only;" *hätta*, "even;" *häm*, "also;" *-ginä*, "only;" *emäs*, "not;" *näfäqät*, "not only;" etc. Likewise, the following postpositions and adverbs may serve in the same function: *täšqäri*, "except," "besides;" *bilän birgä*, "together with," "at the same time;" *ornigä*, "instead of;" *yana*, "further," "more;" *täğin*, "again," "further;" etc. If these signifiers are lacking, the presupposition will be blocked.

The phenomenon of presupposition has a specific relation with the FSP ("Functional Sentence Perspective" - after B. Mathesius). The relation between the FSP and the presupposition is primarily realized through the focus representing the logical stress on a given word in the sentence. For example, in the sentence, "*Men qiziq kitablärni oqiymän*," "I read interesting books," if the word *qiziq* ("interesting") is the focus, it is the *reme*, and the remaining parts are the *theme*. At the same time the focus always lies in the sphere of activity of the presupposition, since a sentence with the intonational center (accent) on the word *qiziq* ("interesting") will have the presupposition, "*bašqä kitablärni oqimäymän*," "I do not read other books." Other devices of actualization (by changing word order, by grammatical means) are also directly linked with the presupposition.

Irrespective of the types of devices through which it is expressed, the reme of utterance is used not in isolation, but posits the existence of its opposites, and this creates their basic presupposition. For example in the sentence "*U kuyläk häm aldi*, "He bought a shirt/dress as well," the particle *häm* ("also") simultaneously implies both the means of actualization and the device of presupposition; the particle, highlighting the word *kuyläk* ("shirt"), at the same time conveys the presupposition, "*bašqä närsä häm aldi*," "He bought other things too;" for the particle *häm* ("and," "also") expresses the inclusion of the concept expressed by *kuyläk* ("shirt," "dress") among other semantically related notions (such as *mäykä*, "vest," *šim*, "trousers," etc.). But in the sentence "*U fäqät kuyläk aldi*," "He bought only a shirt/dress," the particle *fäqät* ("only"), restricting the word *kuyläk* from semantically related concepts, at the same time expresses the presupposition, "*bašqä närsä almädi*," "he did not buy other things." As is evident from the examples, presupposition is determined by concepts which are relatively closely and associatively connected; such concepts are usually termed "opposemes."

The opposemes may be expressed by different means:

1. Only one opposeme is explicitly expressed, and it presupposes the other by association. There may be found various relations between the opposemes, such as copulative, adversative, comparative, gradual, etc. For example:

a) *Koprikni biz qurdik* - "We built a bridge"
b) *Biz fäqät koprik qurdik* - "We built only a bridge"
c) *Biz koprikkinä qurdik* - "We built only a bridge"
d) *Biz koprik häm qurdik* - "We built also a bridge"
e) *Biz yänä koprik qurdik* - "We built another bridge"
f) *Biz hätta koprik qurdik* - "We even built a bridge"

The aforementioned sentences imply the following presuppositions:

a) *Bašqälär qurmädi* - "Others did not build"
b) *Bašqä närsä qurmädik* - "We did not build anything else"
c) *Bašqä närsä qurmädik* - "We did not build anything else"
d) *Basqä närsä häm qurdik* - "We built something else also"
e) *Ilgäri häm koprik qurgänmiz* - "We had built a bridge earlier"
f) *Bašqä närsä häm qurdik* - "We built something else as well"

The sentence elements emphasized posit the opposemes such as *bašqälär* ("others"), *bašqä närsä*, ("something else"), *ilgäri häm*, ("before"), etc.

In the first, second, and third sentences may be observed a distinguishing relation between opposemes, in the fourth and fifth sentences a copulative relation, and in the sixth a gradual relation, etc.

2. Both opposemes have explicit expression, but one of them is a nominalized transform of the predicative expression and is used with

the postpositions *täšqäri*, "except," "besides," *bašqä*, "other than," *bilän birgä*, "together with," "at the same time," *ornigä*, "instead of," or with the negating particles *emäs*, "not," *tugul*, "not," etc. These postpositions and particles serve as signifiers of the presupposition, and their omission blocks the presupposition. For example:

1) *Sendän täšqäri hämmä keldi* - "Except you everybody came"
2) *Oqiš ornigä išlädi* - "Instead of studying he worked"
3) *Oqiš bilän birgä išlädi* - "He combined the study with work"
4) *Kärim emäs Halim keldi* - "Not Karim but Khalim came"
5) *Kärim tugul, hätta Halim keldi* - "Not only Karim but even Holim came"
6) *Näfäqät Kärim, hätta Halim keldi* "Not only Karim, but even Holim came"
7) *Bu qavun emäs, äsäl* - "It is not a melon but honey"

In the first sentence the opposemes are: *sen*, "you," and *hämmä*, "everyone;" in second & third *oqiš*, "studying," and *išlädi*, "worked;" in the fourth, fifth, and sixth, *Kärim* and *Halim*; and in the seventh, *qavun*, "melon," and *äsäl*, "honey."

These sentences imply the following presuppositions:

1) *Sen kelmäding* - "you didn't come"
2) *Oqimädi* - "he (she) didn't study"
3) *Oqidi* - "he (she) studied"
4) *Kärim kelmädi* - "Karim didn't come"
5-6) *Kärim keldi* - "Karim came"
7) *Qavun širinligi äsälgä okhšäydi* - "The melon's sweetness is like honey"

The following relations are observed between the opposemes: in the first sentence, the meaning of the first opposeme is drawn from that of the second one; in the second, the opposemes are posed so that the first opposeme expresses the expected fact, while the other the actual fact; in the third, the meaning of the first opposeme is interlaced with that of the second opposeme; in the fourth, the meaning of the first opposeme is rejected, while the meaning of the second one is confirmed; in the fifth and sixth copulative relations are maintained, and accordingly the meaning of the opposemes is graduated in content, quality, or quantity; and in the seventh, the meaning of the first opposeme is linked to that of the second opposeme.

As is clear from the examples, presuppositions differ as to their characteristic features and the relations observed between the opposemes. Hence there are various classifications of presuppositions proposed by different linguists. According to the characteristics of their manifestation, there are broad, narrow, and linguistic presuppositions (G. V. Gak), semantic and pragmatic presuppositions (E. V. Paducheva), and presuppositions linked to opposemes and those of expectation (Tropova), etc.

Proceeding from the characteristics of their manifestation, we classify presuppositions as either 1) pragmatic or b) linked to opposemes.

The second type is in turn divided into presuppositions of inclusion, of exclusion, of expectation, of existence, of opposition, and of resemblance and comparison.

Thus, in Uzbek, presupposition occurs either in the lexical meaning of a certain syntaxeme (pragmatic presupposition), or with the aid of certain explicity materialized signals (presupposition linked to opposemes), with opposemes playing an essential role in the second type. And naturally, presupposition is part of the semantic structure of the sentence and accordingly comprises one of its aspects worthy of investigation.

A NEW STAGE IN THE DEVELOPMENT OF UZBEK DIALECTOLOGY

A. Shermatov

As a result of an enormous growth of lexical resources and the improvement of its grammatical structure the Uzbek language has been raised to an unprecedented height. Uzbek linguistics took shape and developed as a separate science, and numerous highly qualified Uzbek linguists appeared. It is natural that the problems of the Uzbek national literary language and questions of the culture of native speech have had great importance for Uzbek linguistics. Questions of writing, orthography, orthoepy, general lexical stock, and scientific terminology have taken on great national importance.

At present, very intensive work is being undertaken in Turkic areal linguistics,[1] and toward the comilation of an experimental volume of "A Dialectological Atlas of the Turkic Languages of the USSR."[2] Monographic researches in Uzbek popular dialects, as well as materials collected for cartographic studies of the dialects, have reached such significance that it is now possible to speak of a complete investigation of dialects throughout the territory of Uzbekistan by the method of linguistic geography. "Linguistic maps of contemporary dialects of Turkic languages dialects are, in certain cases, not only the most important source, but indeed the only source for establishing the ancient dialect division of one or another language."[3]

The work on areal linguistics of living Uzbek dialects was begun in the early 1930s. Prof. E. D. Polivanov was the first to point out

[1] N. Z. Gadzhieva, *Problemy tiurkskoi areal'noi lingvistiki* (Moscow, 1975); G. F. Blagova, *Tiurkskoe sklonenie v areal'no-istoricheskom osveshchenii* (Moscow, 1982).

[2] È. R. Tenishev and G. F. Blagova, "Regional'noe koordinirovanie dialektologicheskikh issledovanii - nasushchnaia zadacha tiurkskogo iazykoznaniia v SSSR," *Tezisy dokladov i soobshchenii IX konferentsii po dialektologii tiurkskikh iazykov* (Ufa, 1982), p. 91.

[3] È. R. Tenishev, "Tiurkskaia istoricheskaia dialektologiia i Makhmud Kashgarskii," *Sovetskaia tiurkologiia*, 1973, No. 6, p. 55.

the common Turkic isoglosses in Uzbek dialects.[4] In 1944 Prof. A. K. Borovkov composed the data form called "Questionnaire for the Collection of Materials on Uzbek Dialects."[5] At the beginning of the 1950s Prof. V. V. Reshetov compiled linguistic maps of the Kuramin dialects of Tashkent *oblast'* (40 maps), which, unfortunately, have still not been published.[6] On the basis of materials collected and mapped during 1962-1977, the present author compiled an atlas of the Uzbek popular dialects of Kashkadarya *oblast'*.[7]

Since 1962 the present writer has been engaged in thorough investigation of the structure of Uzbek dialects in their linguistic-geographical aspect, and in the detailed study of the phonetic, morphological, and lexical features of dialects throughout the territory of the Uzbek SSR, through personal observation and field recordings (according to a specially devised programme-questionnaire for an atlas of Uzbek dialects). This research was conducted in 1287 populated areas located within the republic, by listening to 2826 informants (the speech of 428 of them was tape-recorded), identifying the territorial distribution of dialect zones, clarifying the extent of dialects in each group, determining the borders of corresponding isogloss phenomena characteristic of all Uzbek dialects, and demonstrating their areal features; it involved the determination of the linguistic facts associated with each distinct dialect and demonstrating their areal features, and the compilation of a map explaining the distribution of dialect phenomena. In the course of analyzing the material, the influence of the languages of the people of neighboring regions - the Tajik, Turkmen, Kazakh, and Kirgiz SSRs and the

[4] E. D. Polivanov, *Materialy po grammatike uzbekskogo iazyka*, vyp. 1, Vvedenie (Tashkent, 1935), pp. 11-15.

[5] A. K. Borovkov, *Ozbek shevä-lähjälärini tekshirishgä dair säval-jävablär* (Tashkent, 1944).

[6] V. V. Reshetov, "O dielektologicheskom atlase uzbekskogo iazyka," *Tezisy dokladov II regional'nogo soveshchaniia po dialektologii tiurkskikh iazykov* (Kazan', 1958).

[7] A. Shermatov, *Quyi Qäshqädärya ozbek shevälări* (Tashkent, 1972); *idem*, *Uzbekskie narodnye govory Kashkadar'inskoi oblasti* (Tashkent, 1978).

Karakalpak ASSR - on Uzbek dialects was also investigated. Phenomena reflecting various levels of language were also represented on the map. During the cartographic study of dialect data linguistic facts were reflected in really-existing form, and corresponding dialect phenomena were shown in contrast.

The dialect materials are being compared with the facts of dialects of related Turkic languages, with the Tajik literary language and its dialects, and with the sources of the Old Turkic and Old Uzbek languages.

As a result of this prolonged work, the present writer has established that Uzbek dialects, according to their linguistic features, comprise four dialect zones and dialect groups: 1) the Qarluq dialect zone; 2) the Qipchaq dialect zone; 3) the Oghuz dialect zone; 4) a mixed dialect zone.

The QARLUQ DIALECT ZONE is named after one of the old Turkic tribes which was included in the Uzbek people. "The group of the Uzbek people which has preserved the designation "Qarluq" as a clan-tribal name is found primarily in the basins of the Amu Darya's right-hand tributaries. A quite small number of Qarluqs is found along the lower Kashkadarya."[8] A special monograph by K. Shaniiazov is devoted to the origin of the Uzbek-Qarluqs and to their history, economy, and material and intellectual culture.[9] According to N. A. Baskakov's classification, the Qarluq group of Turkic languages was formed in the age of Qarakhanids (10th-11th centuries) as a result of the uniting under the Qarakhanids of peoples with two highly developed cultures - the Uyghur in the east and the Turko-Iranian in the west of Central Asia.[10]

> The close relation of the Turk-Qarluqs to other tribes of the "Turk" group, and in considerable degree to the Uzbeks who had no clan-tribal divi-

[8] B. Kh. Karmysheva, *O nekotorykh drevnikh tiurkskikh plemenakh v sostave Uzbekov* (Moscow, 1960), p. 4.

[9] K. Shaniiazov, *Uzbeki-karluki* (Tashkent, 1964).

[10] N. A. Baskakov, *Vvedenie v izuchenie tiurkskikh iazykov* (Moscow, 1962), p. 131.

> sions, allows us to consider the Turk-Qarluqs as descendants of the Qarluqs of Qarakhanid times. In order to sufficiently ground this hypothesis it is essential to undertake further study of the Qarluqs of southern Tajikistan and those of Afghanistan, and to examine the language of the Qarluqs - that is, that dialect of Uzbek spoken by the Qarluqs of the specified regions.[11]

The investigated population of the Qarluq dialect zone forms the oldest layer in the composition of the Uzbek people; that is, it is the long-standing settled, agricultural, and urban Turkic-speaking population of Central Asia, which had no clan-tribal divisions. In the Qarluq dialect zone are located the *-ye*-pronouncing dialects of rural and urban types: Uzbek dialects of this type belong to the 6th - 7th phonemic dialect, to which the majority of urban Uzbek dialects belong, and to which the Uzbek literary language belongs as well.

Dialects of the QIPCHAQ DIALECT ZONE are spread across vast vast territories of the republic. They exist in all the regions of Uzbekistan as well as outside the republic. It is well-known that all Uzbek dialects of the Qipchaq dialect zone are based on the law of vowel-harmony as far as their vocalism is concerned, while with regard to their consonantism are categorized as *-je-* pronouncing. The Qipchaq dialects of the Uzbek language became the object of scholarly investigation mainly after the Great October Socialist revolution.[12]

[11] B. Kh. Karmysheva, *O nekotorykh drevnikh tiurkskikh plemenakh v sostave uzbekov*, p. 4.

[12] See E. D. Polivanov, "Kazak-naimanskii govor," *Izvestiia AN SSSR*, 1935, 1; V. V. Reshetov, "Klassifikatsiia uzbekskikh govorov Angrenskoi doliny," *Biulleten' AN UzSSR*, 1946, 7; *idem*, "Nekotorye zamechaniia o karakalpakakh Tashkentskogo oazisa i ikh iazyke," *Biulleten' AN UzSSR*, 1947; *idem*, "K voprosu o termine "Kurama" i kuramintsakh," *Biulleten' AN UzSSR*, 1945, 5; U. Tursunov and Kh. Daniyarov, "Ozbek tilidägi singarmonizm häqidä," in *Älisher Nävaiy namidägi ozbek dävlät universitetining äsärläri*, yängi seriya, 91 (Samarkand, 1959); V. Egamov, "Ghälläaral sheväsining bä'zi bir morfologik kategoriyaläri häqidä," *ibid.*; Mukhtar Valiev, *Naimanskii govor uzbekskogo iazyka* (avtoreferat kandidatskoi dissertatsii [hereafter AKD], Samarkand, 1963); T. Mirsagatov, *Kirkskii govor uzbekskogo iazyka* (AKD, Tashkent, 1954); Kh. Daniiarov, *Bakhmal'skii govor uzbekskogo iazyka* (AKD, Moscow, 1955); *idem*, *Ozbek*

In the *-je*-pronouncing dialects of Uzbek, the principle of vowel harmony, which goes back to the oldest periods of Turkic languages, has been preserved in a somewhat distinctive form. According to this feature, the dialects of the Qipchaq dialect zone may be divided into two types: 1) according to their territorial location, and 2) according to their linguistic peculiarities. To the first type belong the Qipchaq dialects found in the territory of Tashkent, Syrdarya, Fergana, Andijan, Bukhara, and Navoi *oblast's*, as well as dialects located near to major cities, which due to their territorial proximity to urban dialects have lost certain features characteristic of *-je*-pronouncing dialects. The second group includes the Qipchaq dialects of the Karakalpak ASSR, and of Khorezm, Samarkand, Kashkadarya, and Syr-darya *oblast's*, in which the influence of urban dialects is only slightly noticeable. Cartographic materials demonstrate that the *-je*-pronouncing dialects located in each territory do not individually constitute independent dialects, but rather form dialect zones and groups of dialects consisting of the totality of corresponding phenomena within the Qipchaq areal of the Uzbek language.

The OGHUZ DIALECT ZONE is located in Urgench, Khiva, Khazarasp, Khanka, Bagat, Yangiarik, Kushkupir, and Shavat *rayons* of Khorezm *oblast'*, and in Karachul, Alat, and Vobkent *rayons* of Bukhara *oblast'* in the Uzbek republic; in the town of Tashauz and in Tashauz and Urgench *rayons* of the Turkmen SSR; in Biruni and Turtkul *rayons* of the Karakalpak ASSR; and in the villages of Mankent, Karabulak, Karamurt, and Kizilkishlak in Sairam *rayon*, and in the villages of Ikan and Karnak in Turkestan *rayon* of Chimkent *oblast'*in the Kazakh SSR.

khälqining shäjarä va sheväläri (Tashkent, 1968); *idem*, *Opyt izucheniia dzhekaiushchikh dialektov v sravnenii s uzbekskim literaturnym iazykom* (Tashkent, 1975); F. Abdullaev, *Ozbek tilining qipchaq sheväsi*, I (Tashkent, 1957); A. Ishaev, *Foneticheskie osobennosti mangitskogo govora uzbekskogo iazyka* (AKD, Tashkent, 1962); *idem*, "Manghit sheväsi morfologiyasidän materiallar," in *Ädäbiyatshunaslik va tilshunaslik mäsäläläri*, IV (1962); F. Abdullaev, "O kipchaksko-oguzskikh sootvetstviiakh p/b, b/m, b/v (po materialam khorezmskikh govorov uzbekskogo iazyka)," in *Voprosy tiurkologii* (Tashkent, 1965); Kh. Babaniiazov, *Fonetiko-morfologicheskie osobennosti kipchakskikh govorov iuzhnogo Khorezma* (AKD, Tashkent, 1966); and others.

The characteristic features of most dialects of the Oghuz dialect zone are: 1) the presence of long vowels;[13] 2) the usage of "ə" instead of "e" in the first syllable of words;[14] 3) correspondence of voiced "g" and "d" to the initial voiceless "k" and "t";[15] 4) the absence of the final "q," "ġ," "k," and "g" after preceding narrow vowels in the definite category of words;[16] 5) the use of the affix -a/-ə in the dative case after consonant stems; 6) the *-yatïr* form of the present-continuous tense of the present moment; 7) the use of the *-jaq/-jək* form of the future tense.[17]

The MIXED DIALECT ZONE: As a result of their living together over the course of many centuries in a specific territory, there emerged in the life of that part of the population of Uzbekistan, Tajikistan, Kazakhstan, Kirgizia, and Turkmenia which spoke two languages in parallel fashion a commonality of territory, language, economy, culture, daily life, and psychological make-up. This led to the creation of a mixed dialect zone in certain territories of Central Asia. As a result of the mixing and mutual penetration of various languages, bilingual dialects were formed historically in the territory of the mixed dialect zone.

Two types of dialect mixing may be observed in the mixed dialect zone: 1) mixing of related Turkic languages (Uzbek-Kazakh, Uzbek-Kirgiz, Uzbek-Turkmen); 2) mixing of unrelated languages (Uzbek and Tajik).

Representatives of the Uzbek-Kazakh bilingual dialects live in Yangiyul, Bostanlik, Srednechirchik, Galaba, and Chinaz *rayons* of Tashkent *oblast'* and in Arnasai, Farish, Gulistan, and Mirzachul *rayons* of Syr-darya *oblast'* in the Uzbek SSR, as well as in

[13] A. M. Shcherbak, *Sravnitel'naia fonetika tiurkskikh iazykov* (Leningrad, 1970), pp. 122-142.

[14] Ghazi Alim, *Ozbek lähjälärining täsnifidä bir täjribä* (Tashkent, 1936).

[15] H. Vámbéry, *Čagataische Sprachstudien* (Leipzig, 1867).

[16] E. D. Polivanov, "Govor kishlaka Kyiatkungrat Shavatskogo raiona," *Trudy UzNIIKS*, vyp. 2 (Tashkent, 1934), pp. 3-22.

[17] F. Äbdulläev, *Ozbek tilining oghuz lähjäsi* (Tashkent, 1978), pp. 10-19.

Turkestan, Sairam, and Lenin *rayons* of Chimkent *oblast'* in the Kazakh SSR.

The dialect zone of the Uzbek-Kirgiz bilingual dialects is found in Osh and Dzhalalabad *oblast's* of the Kirgiz SSR and in Andizhan *oblast'* in the Uzbek SSR. The people of this dialect zone communicate with one another in the two languages in parallel fashion.

Uzbek-Turkmen bilingual dialects are found in Tashauz and Chardzhou *oblast's* in Turkmenia, in the Khorezm oasis and in Beruni and Turtkul *rayons* of the Karakalpak ASSR, and in Karakul *rayon* of Bukhara *oblast'*. Turkmens of the Khorezm oasis and of Chardzhou *oblast'* use the Uzbek language when communicating with Uzbeks;[18] similarly, Uzbeks of Tashauz and Chardzhou *oblast's* in Turkmenia speak Turkmen freely.[19] Conversations are conducted as readily in Turkmen as in Uzbek;[20] to express a given concept the Uzbeks of Turkmenia use Turkmen words, while the Turkmens of the Khorezm oasis use Uzbek words.[21]

Representatives of Uzbek-Tajik bilingual dialects dwell in Bostanlik and Parkent *rayons* of Tashkent *oblast'*; in the Khavas *rayon* of Syr-darya *oblast'*; in Chust and Kasansai *rayons* of Namangan *oblast'*; in the city of Bukhara and in Gidzhduvan, Bukhara and Shafrikan *rayons* of Bukhara *oblast'*; in Samarkand, Kattakurgan and Samarkand *rayons* of Samarkand *oblast'*; in the town of Kasan and in Kassan, Karshi, Ul'ianov, Dekhkanabad, and Guzar *rayons* of Kashkadarya *oblast'*; and in Denou, Uzun, Gagarin, Termez, Sariosia, and Angor *rayons* of Surkhandarya *oblast'*.

One part of the inhabitants of these localities is comprised of people who are by origin Tajiks who speak Uzbek, while the other

[18] *Turkmen dilinin dialektlarining ocherki* (Ashkhabad, 1970), p. 31.

[19] T. Tachmuratov and B. Charyiarov, "Voprosy dvuiazychiia v usloviiakh Turkmenskoi SSR," in *Problemy dvuiazychiia i mnogoiazychiia* (Moscow, 1972), p. 188.

[20] S. Arazkuliev, *Govory turkmen Turtkul'skogo raiona* (AKD, Ashkhabad, 1962), p. 5.

[21] M. Saparov, *Leksiko-semanticheskie osobennosti oguzskogo narechiia uzbekskogo iazyka* (AKD, Tashkent, 1983), p. 7.

part is by origin Uzbek but speaks Tajik.[22]

In his linguistic work entitled *Muḥākamat al-lughatayn* ("Contest of the Two Languages"), ʿAlī-shīr Navāʾī wrote, "These two peoples [Uzbeks and Tajiks] have been strongly mixed with each other in all generations. There is much mixing and communication between the two peoples, and they can speak with and understand each other without hindrance."[23] As is evident, Uzbek-Tajik bilingualism is bilateral process, and has a productive influence not only upon the lexical stock, but on the phonetic and grammatical structures of the two languages as well. In bilingual dialects, lexical, grammatical and phonetic elements represent parallelisms and/or synonyms within the Uzbek and Tajik languages, thereby promoting the further development, and to a certain extent change, of these languages. Thus, for example, one should note as a distinctive characteristic of Tajik among other Iranian languages in the fact that Tajik has an abundance of Turkic, and especially Uzbek, elements; the Uzbek language is likewise distinctive among other related Turkic languages (Kazakh, Kirgiz, Tatar, Karakalpak) by the presence of a whole range of Tajik elements.

The formation of the mixed dialect zone in the territory of Central Asia is the result of the long historical process which began before the consolidation of genetically-related Turkic and ethnically-varied tribal groups comprising the peoples of Central Asia and Kazakhstan. Already in the 11th century, Maḥmūd Kāshgharī noted bilingualism among the Turkic clans and tribes of his time. "The people of Balasaghun speak Sogdian and Turkic, and the inhabitants of Tiraz (Tölös) speak both Sogdian and Turkic."[24]

Besides the literary norms of pronunciation and common linguistic elements characteristic of many dialects of this region, the Uzbek dialects show a quite distinctive differentiation between zones

[22] B. Kh. Karmysheva, *Ocherki ètnicheskoi istorii iuzhnykh raionov Tadzhikistana i Uzbekistana* (Moscow, 1976), p. 122.

[23] Alisher Navoiy, "Suzhdenie o dvukh iazykakh," tr. A. Malekhova, in *Sochineniia v desiati tomakh*, t. I (Tashkent, 1970), p. 110.

[24] Mähmud Kashghäriy, *Devan lughatit turk*, I (Tashkent, 1960), p. 66.

as well. The dialect indications of each zone reflect different historical stages of the linguistic development of dialects in this region.

Thus, the dialect structure of the Uzbek language, which played an important role in the formation not only of the language of the Uzbek people during the pre-national period, but of the old Uzbek literary language as well, has been researched as a whole; the mixing of Uzbek and Tajik, Uzbek and Kazakh, Uzbek and Turkmen, and Uzbek and Kirgiz languages within the republic's territory has been clarified, and the formation and characteristics of bilingual dialects have been investigated.

Consequently, the necessary material for compiling a dialectological atlas of Uzbek popular dialects is fully assembled; the creation of such an atlas marks a new stage in the development of scholarship in Uzbek dialectology and serves as material for the solution of a series of general problems, connected with the historical dialectology and comparative study of Turkic languages, since the dialects of the dialect zones discussed above manifest a system of isoglosses of related and unrelated languages.

SOME LATIN SOURCES ON THE KHANATE OF UZBEK

Denis Sinor

Uzbek, khan of the Golden Horde (r.1313-1342), is an eminent figure in the late medieval history of Central Asia. His renown rests, firstly, on his being the first khan of the Golden Horde to adopt Islam as a state religion, and, secondly, on his being the eponymous ruler of the Uzbek nation. Writing some three hundred years after Uzbek, Abū'l-Ghāzī Bahādur Khan, ruler of the Uzbek khanate of Khiva (r. 1644-1663), described him in glowing terms in his *Genealogy of the Türks*:

> Although this prince was only thirteen years old when he ascended the throne, he held the reins of government with no lesser firmness than did his forefathers. He knew how to recognize and honor with his favors men, each according to his rank and merits. He converted his subjects to Islam and it was thanks to this fortunate prince that all inhabitants of the country had the joy of receiving the light of the Islamic faith. From his time on the *il* [*ulus*] of Jöchi has been called the *il* [*ulus*] of Uzbek, a name which this tribe will keep till Judgment Day.[1]

Abū'l-Ghāzī's lavish praise is justified even by the more measured judgment of modern historians who generally regard him as perhaps the most illustrious ruler of the Golden Horde. The small contribution this paper intends to make to his study will consist of examining a selection of Latin sources relative to his reign. It would appear from their study that this Muslim neophyte, far from being a religious fanatic, has kept alive to a remarkable degree traditional Mongol religious tolerance.

In an article on the Golden Horde written for the 1966 edition of the *Encyclopaedia Britannica*[2] I expressed the view that "The eyes of

[1] P. I. Desmaisons, *Histoire des Mogols et des Tatares par Aboul-Ghâzi Bèhâdour Khan*, 2 vols. (St.Petersburg, 1871), French translation, vol. I, pp. 183-184, text, vol. II, pp. 174-175.

[2] Vol. X, p. 541.

the khans of the Golden Horde were directed southward and eastward rather than toward Europe," an opinion I still hold; however, since in this paper I have to measure the number of words used less strictly than I had for the *Encyclopaedia*, I would like to show that contacts with eastern and western Europe were by no means negligible.

In 1313, the year he assumed power, in a letter addressed to the Mamluk sultan Malik an-Nāṣir, Uzbek boasted that in his land Islam was dominant and that the peoples of the north will be compelled by the force of arms to adopt this religion.[3] His early insistence on conversion alienated some of the Mongol generals who, apparently told him: "Accept our obedience, what does it matter to you what our religion is. Why should we abandon the cult of Chinggis khan for the Arabic religion?"[4]

A very different light is shed on Uzbek's religious policies by a decree (*jarlig*) issued very early in his reign, on March 20, 1314 and known only through a contemporary Latin translation.[5] It should be borne in mind that so far no original, official document of the Golden Horde written during Uzbek's reign or earlier has come to light. Only Russian, Italian or Latin translations have been preserved of these documents originally written either in Turkic or in Mongol.[6] The initial formula of the aforementioned document reads: *In virtute eterni dei & magne maiestatis suffragio, nos Usbek mandamus hec verba nostra*: "In the strength of the eternal God and with the full

[3] Cf. Hammer-Purgstall, *Geschichte der Goldenen Horde in Kiptschak das ist: der Mongolen in Rußland* (Pest, 1824), p. 284.

[4] C. d'Ohsson, *Histoire des Mongols depuis Tchinguiz khan jusqu'à Timour beg ou Tamerlan*, 4 vols. (La Haye et Amsterdam, 1834-1835), vol. IV, p. 573.

[5] Published in Michael Bihl and A.C.Moule, "Tria nova documenta de missionibus Fr. min. Tartariae Aquilonaris annorum 1314-1322", *Archivum Franciscanum Historicum*, XVII (1924), pp. 55-71, commentary pp. 56-58, text p. 65.

[6] On the not fully clarified question concerning the official language of the Golden Horde cf. A. P. Grigor'ev, "Ofitsial'nyi iazyk Zolotoi Ordy XIII-XIV vv.", *Tiurkologicheskii Sbornik 1977* (1981), pp. 81-89, with ample references to earlier works, mainly by the author himself. The article "Evoliutsiia formy adresanta v zolotoordynskikh iarlykakh XIII-XIV vv.," *Vostokovedenie*, 3 (1981), pp. 132-146 seems particularly relevant here, but I have no access to it.

approval of his Majesty, we Uzbek decree these our word," a good rendering of Mongol *Möngke tngri-yin küčün-dür . . . üge manu*: "in the strength of the eternal Heaven [i.e. God] . . . my word." The formula used here is similar to the exordium of the Latin translation of the letter sent to Louis IX of France by Eljigidei, special envoy of the Great Khan Güyük to Baiju, Mongol commander in Transcaucasia. This letter begins with the words: *Per potentiam Dei excelsi . . . verba Elcheltay*: "By the power of God the highest . . . the words of Elcheltay."[7] A sure proof of the originality of Uzbek's letter is the fact that it gives the date of its writing according to the animal cycle (written on the 4th day of the 3rd month of year of the Tiger). In his letter, Uzbek renews the privileges accorded by his predecessors to "the Latin priests who, in their own terms are called the Friars Minor", *[sacerdotes latini qui suo more fratres minores vocantur]* i.e. to the Franciscans, and specifically exempts them from military service, from all types of *corvées* and taxes. Uzbek also decrees that no one should break into, let alone destroy any building owned by Franciscans and forbids any interference with their ringing of the bells. In so doing, Uzbek expressly refers to the precedents established by his predecessors, notably by his uncle the emperor, i.e. Toqtai. In a letter written by a Franciscan in the Genoese colony of Caffa on May 15, 1323 it is reported[8] that the late emperor, i.e. Toqtai, died [in August 1312] a Christian and his three sons had also been Christians but that two of them apostatized.[9] There might be some doubt concerning the Christianity of Toqtai himself but the conversion of the queen mother Theodotelia, of the empress Kerley, and of her three sons can be taken for granted.[10] According to another docu-

[7] See Paul Pelliot, "Les Mongols et la Papauté", *Revue de l'Orient Chrétien*, XXVIII (1931), p. 21.

[8] Michael Bihl - A.C.Moule, "De duabus Epistolis Fr. Minorum Tartariae Aquilonaris an. 1323", *Archivum Franciscanum Historicum*, XV (1923), p. 111.

[9] On the name Toqtai and the question of his possible conversion cf. Paul Pelliot, *Notes sur l'histoire de la Horde d'Or* (Paris, 1949), particularly p. 71.

[10] Cf. Girolamo Golubovich, *Biblioteca bio-bibliografica della Terra Sancta e dell'Oriente Francescano*, 5 vols. (Quaracchi-Firenze, 1906-1927) [henceforth: Golubovich] III, p. 175, and Jean Richard, *La Papauté et les missions d'Orient au Moyen Age (XIIIe-XVe siècles* (Rome, 1977), p. 157.

ment[11] written in the 1320s Coktogani (Toktogani?), a son of the emperor Toqtai[12] (whose name is also spelled this way), was buried in the church of St.John of Sarai, the capital of the Golden Horde.

Over the years, Uzbek's attitude towards Christians remained ambivalent, determined perhaps by the behavior of the Italians who constituted the majority of non-native Christians. In 1316 Uzbek allowed the reconstruction of the Genoese colony of Caffa which had been destroyed in 1307 at the orders of Toqtai (1291-1312), who was greatly irritated by the continuing trade in children of which the Genoese were guilty.[13] Uzbek's reputation among contemporary western specialists of the region was varied. The Dominican William of Adam in his voluminous memorandum *De modo Sarracenos extirpandi*, "How to root out the Muslims", written in 1317, avers that Uzbek - not mentioned by name but referred to as "emperor of the northern Tartars" (*imperator Tartarorum aquilonis*) - is hostile to and persecutes the Christians as shown by his order that all bells be removed from the churches. According to William, Uzbek did so at the behest of the Sultan of Egypt.[14]

The ringing of the bells seems to have been a perennial problem caused, one might guess, not so much by Uzbek's preferences but by the need of maintaining peace among a mixed population which may have viewed the use of bells as a provocative action. (It is to avoid such risks that in the United States Roman Catholic churches traditionally refrain from ringing the bells.) On February 5, 1318 Pope John XXII wrote a letter to "His Magnificence Usbek, emperor of the Tatars" (*Magnifico viro Usbeck imperator Tartarorum)* to be carried to Sarai by Jerome of Catalonia, bishop of Caffa. By its introductory words the letter struck an optimistic note. *Laetanter audivimus*, "We have heard with pleasure," writes the pope, all the good things Uzbek

[11] Golubovich II, p. 79 f.

[12] See Pelliot, *Horde d'Or*, p. 71, and Richard, *La Papauté*, p. 157.

[13] Golubovich III, p.174.

[14] *Recueil des historiens des Croisades. Documents arméniens* II, (Paris, 1906), pp. 530-531 and also Golubovich III, p. 180 where the abduction of children is also mentioned.

had done for the Christians and he thanks the khan for the protection accorded to them. Yet, he calls the khan's attention to the interdiction to ring their bells which, for about three years, had been placed upon Christians. The pope attributes such action not to Uzbek's own initiative but to unspecified "enemies of Christ" who had induced him to take such measures.[15] The request did not produce the expected results and five years later, on September 23, 1323, the pope sent another *Laetanter audivimus* letter, almost verbatim identical with the one sent in 1318. In this brief the pope asked Uzbek to render justice to the Christians living in Soldaia (Sudak in the Crimea) persecuted by Muslims who had turned churches into mosques, and reiterated his plea to Uzbek for permission to use church bells.[16]

Various difficulties notwithstanding, great religious tolerance was a hallmark of Uzbek's rule. This attitude is well described in a letter written by the Hungarian Franciscan Iohanca and sent sometime in 1320 to the minister general of his order.

The friar describes in vivid terms his and his companions' missionary activities and ascribes their success to the attitude of the Tatars who "could not care less to what religion someone belongs as long as he performs the required services, pays tributes and taxes and satisfies his military obligations according to their laws." So it happens that a Christian serf is better off than his master and acts not so much as a serf but rather as an ally and he goes with his master to war against the Muslims.[17]

One of the many Franciscan friars active in the Kipchak land was Elias of Hungary, who became a trusted friend of Uzbek and also of his son Tini Beg[18] to the point that Uzbek entrusted him with a mis-

[15] Text in Golubovich III, p. 178.

[16] Golubovich III, p. 179.

[17] Fr.Iohanca's letter was published in Bihl - Moule "Tria nova..." (see above, note 5), pp. 65-70. This important document would deserve a complete, careful translation into a modern language.

[18] Tini Beg's rule was extremely short; following his father's death he was promptly murdered by his brother Jani Beg. On these events see Bertold Spuler, *Die Goldene Horde. Die Mongolen in Rußland*, Second edition (Wiesbaden, 1965), p. 99.

sion to Pope Benedict XII (1334-42). It could be that the letters carried by this embassy were sent in response to a letter dated June 13, 1338 carried to Uzbek by John of Marignolli in which the pope had asked Uzbek to send him his ambassadors.[19]

Further down I will come back to John of Marignolli, but first let me hark back to John of Monte Corvino the first Catholic archbishop of Peking (Khanbalik) who died in 1330 or somewhat earlier. His immediate successor, the Minorite Nicholas, appointed in 1333 by John XXII, was travelling by land on his way to China and carried with him a letter dated October 1 of that year, addressed to Uzbek, "ruler of Gazaria" in which the pope recommends Nicholas to his goodwill while urging the khan to convert to Christianity.[20] Nicholas probably never reached China but there is evidence of his presence in Almalik.[21] In the meanwhile, the flock of the late John of Monte Corvino sent to Avignon a delegation led by a certain Andrew (Andrew the Frank in one of the manuscripts) accompanied by an uncertain number of companions,[22] some of them certainly Alans. One of the letters they carried,[23] signed by a number of Catholic Alans, urged the pope to appoint a successor to John of Monte Corvino. Their names, distorted in the document, can nevertheless be traced in Chinese sources.[24] The delegation also presented to the

[19] Cf. Golubovich IV, p. 252.

[20] Published in J.H.Sbaralea - C.Eubel (eds.), *Bullarium Franciscanum*, vol. V (1898), pp. 557-558.

[21] Cf. A. C. Moule, *Christians in China before the Year 1550* (London, 1930), pp. 196-197, and also Jean Richard, *La Papauté*, pp. 152-153.

[22] One Vatican manuscript speaks of fifteen, while a Paris manuscript gives five as their number. In an entry of the papal treasury dated June 9, 1338, mention is made of garments given to eight envoys of the Great Khan. Cf. K. H. Schäfer, *Die Ausgaben der Apostolischen Kammer unter Benedikt XII., Klemens VI, und Innocenz VI, (1335-1362)* (Paderborn, 1914), p. 80. According to I. de Rachewiltz, *Papal Envoys to the Great Khans* (Stanford, 1971), p. 187, and Richard, *La Papauté*, p. 153, Andrew was also known as Andalo of Savignone.

[23] Golubovich IV, pp. 250-251 gives the text of the Paris ms.

[24] This was first noted by Paul Pelliot, "Chrétiens d'Asie Centrale et d'Extrême-Orient", *T'oung Pao*, XV (1914), p. 642. The question was taken up again by Herbert Franke, "Das 'himmlische Pferd' des Johann von Marignola",

pope a second letter, this one by the last Yuan emperor Toghan Temür (Shun-ti, 1333-1368).[25] Written in July 1336 in Khanbalik, it is certainly genuine, dated as it is according to the calendar of the twelve animals (year of the Rat), but we have only the Latin translation.[26] The original was probably in Mongol though the exordium *In fortitudine Omnipotentis Dei*, "by the strength of God almighty," is not followed by some rendering of an expected Mongol *üge manu*, "my word". The letter of the Alan "princes" (the title is not used by themselves but only by the pope in his response) begins with the same words. In his short letter Toghan Temür recommends to the Pope "the Alans my servants and your Christian sons" and asks him to send "from where the sun goes down, horses and other marvels" (*alia mirabilia*). It was in response to these requests - coming from the Great Khan and from the Alans -that in the fall of 1338 Benedict XII sent off the mission of John of Marignolli.

John, who refers to himself as John of Florence, set out on his journey in company of three other friars, Nicholas Boneti, Nicholas de Molano (presumably Italians) and Gregory of Hungary. John was not the original leader of the mission which has become well known because of his description of it. The first name mentioned in the papal instructions[27] given on October 31, 1338, to the departing friars is that of Nicholas Boneti "professor of Sacred Theology" who, presumably, was the senior member of the mission. For reasons unknown, from Constantinople he returned to Europe. The friars

Archiv für Kulturgeschichte, 50 (1968), pp. 33-40, specifically pp. 34-35. Interestingly, neither Pelliot nor Franke have attempted to establish the original, Alan, forms of these names.

[25] Golubovich IV, p. 250. The study of this important document lies outside the scope of this study. For further references see Richard, *La Papauté*, p. 153, and also I. de Rachewiltz, *Papal Envoys*, pp. 187-192.

[26] Golubovich IV, p. 250; translation in Sir Henry Yule, *Cathay and the Way Thither*, new edition revised by Henri Cordier, 4 vols. (London, 1913-1916), III, pp. 180-181.

[27] For the text see L. Wadding, *Annales Minorum*, 3rd edition, vol. VII (Firenze, 1932), pp. 253-255.

carried with them a number of letters of recommendation, virtually with the same wording, including one to Uzbek, dated October 31, 1338.[28] The embassy was well provided with the wherewithal necessary for the long journey. On November 21 Benedict's treasury paid 1,500 florins for their travel expenses.[29] The four Franciscans left Avignon in December and, because of a lengthy stay in Naples, arrived in Constantinople as late as the first of May. Continuing their journey, the friars crossed the Black Sea in eight days and reached Caffa whence they continued by land to Saray.[30] They were very well received by Uzbek. In John of Marignolli's words:

> ...we reached the first emperor of the Tartars, Usbeg, and presented a letter, robes, a war-horse [*dextrarius*], *cytiac*, and the Pope's gifts. And, after the winter, well fed, handsomely dressed and rewarded, and provided by him with horses and expenses, we arrived at Almalik of the Middle Empire . . ."[31]

Let me mention that John of Marignolli and his companions carried with them also a letter to Chansi addressed as *imperator Tartarorum de Medio Imperio*, "emperor of the Chagatay khanate," verbatim identical with that sent to Uzbeg. The gift of a horse to an Inner Asian potentate might at first seem strange but, as we have seen, Toghan Temür had expressly asked for them, together with other "marvels." Apparently John had with him several of these

[28] The brief *Dudum ad notitiam*, in Wadding VII, pp. 256-257.

[29] Cf. K. H. Schäfer, *op.cit.*, p. 76.

[30] On their itinerary see Yule, *Cathay*, III, p. 210 and Golubovich IV, p. 262 f.

[31] Golubovich IV, p. 272. English translations of this letter were made by Moule, *Christians in China*, p. 255, and by Yule, *Cathay*, III, pp. 211-212. The friars carried with them also a letter to Chansi "imperator Tartarorum de Medio Imperio", i.e. the Chagatay khanate, verbatim identical with that sent to Uzbek. *Citiacam (var. tyriacam, theriacam)* was probably a medicine or some special liquor. Moule suggests that it was a drink made of fruits.

steeds which on 19th August 1342 in Shang-tu he presented to the Great Khan himself. They became known in China as the "heavenly horses," celebrated in painting and poems.[32]

The favorable and generous reception given to John of Marignolli is proof that Uzbek paid serious attention to his ties with the papacy. Sometime, probably in the spring or early summer of 1340, Uzbek sent an embassy to the pope. His envoys were a certain Petranus de Lorca, Albert his companion, and Elias of Hungary. The letters they carried do not seem to have survived but we know the names of the messengers from the pope's reply. In the early fall of 1340 the aforementioned Elias of Hungary was entrusted with the task of carrying three briefs dated from Avignon August 17, 1340 and destined respectively to Uzbek, to his wife Taydola, and to his son Tini beg. One among them, addressed to Uzbek and beginning with the words *Laetanter et benigne recipimus*, "We received with joy and benevolence," is of particular importance.[33]

In this brief Benedict XII thanks Uzbek for his goodwill towards Christians and for the generous hospitality offered to John of Marignolli. He also refers to the conflicts opposing Uzbek to Poland and to Hungary and urges the khan to desist from such actions. These words were, perhaps, somewhat disingenuous since just a few days earlier, on August 1, the pope had called on the Polish bishops to declare a Crusade against the Tatars and offered plenary indulgence to those helping the Polish king Casimir III (1334-1342) in his war against Uzbek.[34] Of particular interest for the history of Uzbek's rule is the pope's reference in this letter to an attempt that had been made on Uzbek's life. His palace had been set on fire and, although some had accused the Christians of fomenting the plot, Uzbek continued to show goodwill toward them. We learn also that only three Christians took part in the conspiracy which, to my admittedly limited knowledge, is not mentioned in any other source. Not unexpectedly, Benedict used the occasion to remind Uzbek of the brevity of human

[32] See Franke, "Das 'himmlische Pferd'," cited in note 24. John of Marignolli reached Khanbalik in 1342 and spent there three or four years.

[33] Golubovich IV, p. 227, also Wadding VII, p. 269.

[34] Cf. Spuler, *Goldene Horde*, p. 98.

life and the incertitude about our exit from it and suggested that this may be an opportune time for Uzbek to embrace Christianity.[35]

***

This selection of references to Uzbek culled from Latin is, at best, but a footnote to Uzbek's history. Most of these data had been known for centuries and were used repeatedly by ecclesiastic historians. I did little else than to regroup them from a different point of view and, here and there, add a few comments of my own. The compartments of history are leaky vessels, and no one investigation is independent of any other.

[35] On this see Richard, p.160.